APPENDIX B

THE

"LOOK OF THE PERIOD"

AN

ILLUSTRATED REVIEW

Who wore what?

Women's Wear
1861-1865

by Juanita Leisch

THOMAS PUBLICATIONS
Gettysburg PA 17325

For Mom and Dad
and Mrs. Loope —
who encouraged me to reason

Who wore what?

Women's Wear
1861-1865

TABLE OF CONTENTS

❖ ACKNOWLEDGEMENTS ❖

I'd like to extend my most grateful thanks to the following people for their contributions to this book. To my parents, who are always more supportive than I deserve. To Les, who is still listening, commenting, and making suggestions. To all those who have listened to my presentations and made suggestions and comments. And, to the collectors who have offered their photographs for incorporation to the survey.

I would also like to thank the following individuals in particular: Lia Anderson, Vida Jones, Judith Martin, Laura McVey, Casey O'Connor, Dori Toepfer, Belinda Womack, and one very special anonymous collector.

Thanks also to Elizabeth Pidgeon-Ontis for the line drawings, Shawn Heiges for the chapter-divider artwork, Chris Nelson for the use of the photo that appears on this page, Mike McAfee for permission to reprint his woman-in-undress photograph, Mary Ellen Urbanski for permitting me to photograph her (spectacular!) bonnets, and to Mike O'Donnell for photographing the originals seen in this book. And finally, to Dean Thomas and his staff of experts at Thomas Publications who handled the design and editing of the book.

As always, I would also like to thank God for making all of this possible.

To all those who read with open minds and discuss with open mouths, take this information and, agreeing or disagreeing, add to the body of research. I wish you very happy hunting!

There are a number of books that describe the variety of clothing styles worn by women in America during the Civil War period. Unfortunately, these inventories of style have led to the erroneous impression that any woman might have worn any of the styles, and in any combination. Women today don't dress interchangeably. Some women wear styles that other women never adopt—or that they wear only after significant "toning down." It seems improbable that all women of other eras dressed identically, so this study was devised to examine which women wore which of the styles.

First, why bother with a study of this type? What, really, is the problem if 90% of those who portray women of the Civil War period wear a hair style that was worn by fewer than 2% of women in that period? This is exactly the type of problem that must be addressed. Historical accuracy is fact, not fiction, but all too often people are more influenced by their own opinions and preferences rather than factual information. Understanding and portraying women of the past as individuals, rather than as clones of each other, is the first step to realistic impersonations. One case-in-point, recognizable to everyone, is as follows.

Modern Americans who have seen the movie *Gone With the Wind* often come away with an impression of Scarlett O'Hara as a smart-mouthed, head-strong vixen. (Remember how she argued with Mammy before the picnic, and insisted on wearing that immodest, low-neck, short-sleeved dress?) When a modern viewer is alerted to the characteristics of children's clothing in the period, they often come away with a slightly different opinion of Scarlett. The picnic dress, with its short sleeves and wide neckline, was a child's dress. Mammy was encouraging her to dress *more* like an adult. Scarlett was a slightly spoiled child.

At living history events, reenactors sometimes portray a society in economic distress because it brings credibility and logic to scenarios depicting the effects of the war on civilians. Although this does help draw attention to the characters, it is not the *only* way that history should be represented. Instead, portraying women with varying dress styles helps to avoid the all-too-common tendency of imagining all women of the past as one-dimensional ornaments.

But the variations are effective only if the exceptions stand out; if most people portray the norm. Scarlett's dress stood out at the picnic because she was the only person wearing the wide neckline and short sleeves. By the same token, a woman who dresses "young" by wearing a shirt and skirt in this period will only appear young if other women are wearing more mature styles, with bodices and skirts of the same fabric. The exception only stands out when there is a "norm" to contrast it against.

The economic hardships which women encountered—and overcame—can and should be portrayed if women are to be understood and appreciated. But if everyone, or no one, portrays women at the height of fashion, the depth and variety of experiences are obscured. Thus, this book contains information on the economy of the period and the way in which clothing exhibited economic restrictions, as well as other variations, and who wore them.

A Note on Sources

There are several challenges to obtaining reliable sources of information for a study of this type. Keeping in mind that consistency and valid conclusions must be maintained throughout, the sources should be ones that (1) are readily available; (2) provide information that is pure and accurately dateable to the Civil War period; (3) permit the observation of who wore the clothing; (4) provide details of style and dress.

Obtaining sources that were readily available for use was particularly important because this survey began as a project while I was house-bound with a fractured vertebrae, so I started with my own collection of photographs and period clothing. Since regaining mobility, the survey has been expanded to include additional collections. I used studio photographs and based my conclusions on the information that I gathered from them.

The studio photographs met all of the elements required for making a detailed, accurate study of style and dress of women in the Civil War period. There exist tens of thousands of formal, portrait-type photographs that were made when people visited their local studio and posed for a photograph.

The photographs I used, called cartes de visite (CDVs), were printed on paper and glued to pieces of cardstock approximately 2 1/2 by 4 inches in size. The manufacturing and selling of this cardstock quickly became a national industry dominated by a few suppliers who distributed to the numerous photographers. These manufacturers changed their styles of cardstock about every year, which enables historians to date CDVs with relative ease.

Initially, cardstock was a white or cream color and about as thick as the cover of a modern-day paperback book. They were flexible and generally had square corners. Some were decorated with single or double borders of gold, black, or red ink. As time went on, the thickness of the cards was increased, making them far less flexible. Their sizes also increased, and some were made in a variety of colors, including gold, pink, and black. *Rule of thumb*: A carte de visite on cardstock as thick and stiff as a credit card post-dates the Civil War.

Other features that permit the precise dating of CDVs are the various advertising marks that were placed on the back of cardstocks by photographers. In earlier years, these backmarks were rather small and plain, and generally consisted of a printed name and address of the studio across the short dimension of the card in a small, plain typeface. The advertisements seldom occupied even half the empty space on the back of the card. As time went on, the photographers created larger and more elaborate advertisements, even turning the print to extend diagonally or lengthwise on the card. *Rule of thumb*: If the cardstock is heavy and the backmark is positioned diagonally or vertically on the card, the CDV definitely post-dates the Civil War.

A third way to date CDVs relies on the enthusiasm of the government for (revenue from) photography. Both the U.S. and C.S. governments required photographers to pay licensing fees, and to renew these licenses on an annual basis. CDVs can be dated with some certainty to the period during which photographers paid licensing fees to be in business at a specific location. Since photographers—even those who stayed in business throughout the duration of the war—frequently moved their studios, licensing records sometimes allow the dating of a photograph to within months (see Ross Kelbaugh, *Introduction to Civil War Photography*, 11).

Finally, the U.S. government provided yet another means of dating photographs: Between September 1864 and September 1866, the U.S. government raised money for the payment of war debts by collecting a tax on photographs, playing cards, and a number of other goods. A stamp was affixed to the back of photographs indicating that the tax had been paid. *Rule of thumb*: Photographs with revenue stamps date no earlier than the last eight months of the war.

A Note on Content

Studio photographs are dateable, but do they provide accurate information on "Who (really) Wore What"? The answer is "yes." Photography was a relatively new science in the 19th century, and with the popular new technique of making albumen photographs on paper, people could have multiple prints made from a single negative. As literature, newspapers, songs, and signs extolled the value of having (and distributing) one's photograph, it seemed that every crossroads village had a studio. And, prices were cheap enough that most people could afford to have a photograph made.

Since having one's photograph made was a much-discussed event, studio photographs have been criticized as a source of information about clothing with the theory that people did not dress in their "normal" clothing to have their photograph made. What good is it to know "Who Wore What" if "they" were mostly photographed in formal attire? Evidence indicates that, in fact, "they" were normal people who wore ordinary clothing when having their photograph made.

Americans today have specialty outfits that are closeted nearly all of the time, brought out only for special occasions. Photographs taken of us as we set out on our ski vacations show us in clothing that we do not normally wear. This

(Above) A plain and simple backmark, typical of earlier CDVs.

(Right) A more elaborate backmark printed vertically on a post-Civil War photo.

(Far right) CDV backmark with revenue stamp.

example does not apply to most people of the Civil War. Military historians examine studio photographs for information on uniforms of the period. They recognize that the way in which the clothing was worn might have varied in the field—with buttons of the coat undone, or the coat even removed—but they do not believe that the average soldier had enough uniforms to reserve one for ceremonial or photographic occasions. The same is true of civilians.

Americans had far fewer sets of clothing than we do today. With the possible exception of the "upper crust" and celebrities, women simply did not have the luxury of owning wearable outfits that they did not use. In an era when material was relatively expensive, women thought in terms of their next iteration of an outfit, rather than their next new outfit. An unused outfit was probably being taken apart and remade into something else. A "best" dress was so designed because it was newer than the others, or had the best collar (temporarily) basted to it. However, with that collar removed, and an apron added, it was just another dress to wear during the day's activities. Studio photographs show normal clothing, not specialty clothing, for the simple reason that most people did not own anything else.

Thousands of contemporary accounts include comments by those who mention in passing the taking of photographs. "Fanny would like a full length picture of you. The last one you sent is not flattering." A small portion of these mention, with some specificity, "had my photograph made in my new dress," or "The unit received new coats today. I had my photograph taken while wearing mine." The comments lead to the impression that, in fact, wearing new clothes while having a photograph made was an event worthy of note. The unstated, the norm, was to wear ordinary clothing.

Despite all this, there were some Americans who did not have the resources that were available to most Americans and who never sat for photographs. The information in this photograph-based study is still relevant. Evidence—and logic—indicate that a poorer person would exhibit more of the variations discussed in the "Economic Variations" section. And, since they obtained new clothing less frequently, would dress less fashionably (and more like someone in an older age group) than richer contemporaries.

A Note on Methods

What good is it to survey only a sampling of photographs if we cannot see every photograph ever made, and we know that some people never had their photographs taken? Nearly all research, particularly social and cultural, is based on sampling valid data and drawing conclusions about the whole from a part.

In preparing this book, precautions were taken to ensure that conclusions were based on evidence, not pre-conceived notions. In choosing studio photographs as a source of infor-mation, I was able to examine details of dress—"what," and to cross-reference that information against a variety of demographic characteristics—"who." I attempted to make this demographic data as objective as possible. Each chapter begins with a photograph illustrating the "norm" or common manner of wearing a style or accessory. The other photographs and illustrations represent variations in construction and style that were typical of the Civil War period, as well as pre- and post-war variations.

In separating urban photographs from rural photographs, I wanted to capture the women who had access to the goods and services available in major cities. It is certainly true that some of the photographs with urban backmarks might actually depict women who came to the city and had their photographs made, but who actually lived outside the city. These women, whose photographs had urban backmarks, were counted among the urban. Presumably, the type of woman who would patronize an urban photographer rather than one in or close to her own rural area is the same sort of woman who would patronize urban dressmakers.

This survey admittedly includes more information from northern than southern sources. However, it is noted that the photographs with southern backmarks exhibited clothing characteristics which were consistent with the general conclusions. The economic realities of life in the south require that those portraying southerners take particular note of differences between urban and rural, and of economic variations.

The ages of the women in the study were estimated by superficial examination only. The true, exact ages of the women were not essential to the accuracy of the text, and it was decided to group them into four sets: 15-25, 26-40, 41-65, and 66+. This allowed acceptable conclusions to be drawn from the available details.

CDVs provide empirical data on the location and age of the wearers, but it was not always possible to identify the economic status of the individuals by their photographs. In determining the economic influences on the styles of dress, diaries and journals augmented the photographic research. These sources provided valuable first person accounts that described economic situations.

Overall, my research has led to the conclusion that there was a common "look" of the period shared by most women. Variations on the "look" were adopted by women according to their age and varied widely from the very young to the elderly. It is hoped that this information on the "look" and the age-based variations on that look will be put to use by those who wish to accurately portray American history of the Civil War period.

PART

1

WOMEN'S WEAR

Overall Appearance

Individual Appearance

Economic Influence on Appearance

OVERALL APPEARANCE

Any effort to reproduce the "look" of women in the Civil War period requires a leap of faith: that there was a specific appearance for the women in that period. Accurate efforts also require the conviction that reproducing the "look" is more important than maintaining the vestiges of a 1990s image (the bangs *must* come off the forehead).

For example, if it were the year 2125, and you were assigned the task of outfitting a mannequin to represent "the American Woman of the 1990s," would you be capable of designing an image that would be representative of most women? The answer is probably "yes."

In creating the "look of the 1990s," you might just dress the mannequin in a pair of pants, and a shirt. You would fix her hair in a short (by historical standards) haircut, wash and style it so that it looks "clean," and frame the face with the cut or curl of the hair. With makeup, you would emphasize the hollows of her cheeks, darkness of her eyelashes, and the color of her lips.

While your mannequin might be representative of the 1990s, it would not match each and every woman because women do not dress identically. However, women in the 1990s do (subconsciously, at least) dress in conformance with a cultural ideal that says women should look slender, and their clothing should be practical and comfortable.

Similarly, women of the Civil War period dressed to conform with a cultural ideal. In their culture, clothing was designed to help them look narrow at the waist, and wide at the face, hips, and shoulders. 1860s women were less concerned about overall slenderness, and even used foundation garments that added to the width of their silhouette (something that women of the 1990s scrupulously avoid). Nearly all lines of their garments served to emphasize the narrowness of the waist, in contrast to the width of other parts of their body, and nearly all lines of their garments directed the attention to the center front of the waist. These, then, are some of the characteristics that make up the overall "look" of women in the Civil War period:

Hair—Women of the Civil War period wanted their faces to look full and round. The hair was styled flat on top, with any fullness at the sides and back, not the top. It was less important that the hair look "clean" (dry) than that it be controlled. Whether confined in rolls, braids, or curls, the ends of the individual hairs were generally hidden from view. Makeup, when worn, emphasized fullness in the cheeks.

Dresses—were constructed with definite waist seams at the natural waistline. The waist was further emphasized through the use of belts (and jewelry worn at the waist).

Bodices—were constructed so that seam lines (like the arm-hole seams), and any trim lines added width to the shoulders, but not the waist.

Collars, cuffs and chemisettes—were worn as practical, as well as decorative, elements. They were relatively plain, and were constructed of washable, starchable cotton fabrics.

Skirts—were gathered or pleated so that the fabric hung in diagonal lines radiating out from the center front. This differs from post-war skirts, which were often flat at the front.

The photo below shows the most common characteristics of clothing seen on women of the Civil War period:

Cap:	None
Net:	None
Hair:	Confined
Ensemble:	One fabric
Bodice:	Fitted
Neckline:	Jewel
Broach/Tie:	Broach
Collar:	Lays down
Collar size:	Less than 2.5"
Collar fabric:	White cloth
Sleeves:	2-pc "coat"
Cuff/Undersleeves:	Present
Waistline:	Straight
Belt:	50/50 (possible)
Waist treatment:	Knife pleats
Skirt length:	Off ground

INDIVIDUAL APPEARANCE

An obstacle that is encountered when dealing with the clothing design of a specific time period involves age differences. It is common for women to dress similar to others in their same age group, and much different from those in other age groups, even though they all belong to the same culture. Books written in the past regarding the clothing styles of the Civil War period have provided broad inventories of the fashion trends of the day. Unfortunately, this has led to the erroneous conclusion that any combination of those styles would yield an accurate representation of the time period. We now know, through the use of documented historical text and photographs, that reproducing the "look" of the Civil War period requires knowing not only *what* styles were worn in the period, but *who* wore them, and why.

Women, in both the 1990s and the 1860s, tend to dress in a manner that conforms with the way they learned to dress in early life. For example, women who did not wear bikini underwear when young are unlikely to switch to that style when they get older. It is not surprising, then, that in the 1860s, women of older age groups continued to wear styles that had passed out of fashion, while some styles being worn by young adults had not yet come into use by older women.

For the purpose of this book, the population was divided into four age groups: 15-25, 26-40, 41-65, and 66+. These ages were determined by how old the women in photographs appeared to the 20th century eye. No attempt was made to determine the actual age of the subjects, or to adjust for the widely-held theory (myth?) that women in history generally looked older than women their same age in later centuries.

Young women (in the 15-25 age group) sometimes wore dresses that resembled those that they wore as children. These had wide, boat necklines (which modern eyes sometimes confuse with the evening gown necklines of adults in the period). Occasionally, they also had the short sleeves of children's garments. For accessories, they sometimes wore the short, choker or pendant necklaces worn by children.

Older women (66+) sometimes wore dresses which resembled those which were fashionable in the 1840s. They may have "V" necklines filled in to the nape of the neck with partial blouses known as chemisettes. Some wore caps on their heads that covered the crown of the head all the way to the ears, which were more popular in the earlier part of the century.

Younger Women

Most common characteristics of clothing worn by younger women of the Civil War period:

Cap:	None
Net:	May
Hair:	Confined
Ensemble:	Two fabrics
Bodice:	Shirt
Neckline:	Jewel
Broach/Tie:	Tie
Collar:	Lays down
Collar size:	Less than 1"
Collar fabric:	White cloth
Sleeves:	2-pc "coat"
Cuff/Undersleeves:	Present
Waistline:	Straight
Belt:	Yes
Waist treatment:	Knife pleats
Skirt length:	Off ground

Older Women

Most common characteristics of clothing worn by older women of the Civil War period:

Cap:	May
Net:	None
Hair:	Confined
Ensemble:	One fabric
Bodice:	Fan, mod fan
Neckline:	Jewel
Broach/Tie:	Broach
Collar:	Lays down
Collar size:	Less than 4"
Collar fabric:	White cloth/lace
Sleeves:	2-pc "coat"
Cuff/Undersleeves:	Present
Waistline:	Straight
Belt:	No
Waist treatment:	Knife pleats
Skirt length:	Off ground

ECONOMIC INFLUENCE ON APPEARANCE

Women of the 1860s also dressed in conformance with the economy of their time. In the 1990s, time is more expensive than material, so we tend to skimp on labor, and waste material. 1990s seamstresses making 1860s costumes tend to use too many fabrics (and to treat fabric as a disposable good), and they tend to spend too little time with labor-intensive projects (like making and applying bias-cut strips of the dress fabric itself). These are some of the characteristics of period clothing that illustrate the influence of the economy on style and materials:

Fabric—was conserved when making garments by "piecing" together smaller pieces (matching the prints), and using these pieced bits of fabric in inconspicuous places.

Expensive gowns—were often made of fabrics with large prints. The necessary waste in matching such prints made the use of extremely large prints a sign of affluence.

Less expensive dresses—were most often made of solid fabrics or those with small prints so that fabric could be pieced without wasting fabric when matching prints.

Working clothes—were often made of reversible, solid fabrics or fabrics with woven-in prints that had no "up" or "down," so that the fabric panels (especially those in the skirt) could be turned upside down and inside out to re-use the fabric when a garment became faded.

Necklines—were protected from the wear and filth of the neck with fabric collars that attached to the inside of the neckline.

Sleeves—were protected from the wear and filth of the wrist with fabric cuffs that attached to the inside of the sleeve, or with undersleeves worn inside the sleeve.

Skirt panels—were constructed so the fabric could be re-used. Skirts with center front panels fastened at the side front, so that the opening was in a seam, not cut into the panel.

Hems—were constructed of scrap fabrics so that good dress fabrics were turned under less than an inch, with the rest of the hem made of a facing. With expensive dress fabrics, hem tapes were affixed around the edge of the hem to protect it from wear. Dresses made of translucent gauzes and other lightweight fabrics were hemmed with the dress fabric itself so that the drape of the skirt was not affected by a hem facing.

Period photograph of a woman which illustrates more of a concern for thrift as opposed to extravagance.

Some typical characteristics of clothing of less affluent women included those with solid white fabric collars, cuffs, and undersleeves. Fabric was pieced together for cutting pattern pieces, and prints with small repeats, or solid fabrics, especially those which could be turned, were essential to allow the material to be re-used in another form. The goal was to prolong the life of the material for as long as possible.

Women of a more wealthy background, on the other hand, tended to not use as many precautions in preserving material. Some characteristics of their clothing included floor length skirts with trains; the use of fabric with large prints; the use of dress fabric for facings (as in the hem of a pagoda sleeve); skirts that were patterned into a special shape; fabrics printed for a specific use; and prints with a "right" and "wrong" side which prevented turning them, were common attributes that prevented re-using the material.

PART

2

HEAD TO HEMLINE

NETS

late-war and post-war photographs show older women wearing the hairnets which, during the war, were generally seen on younger women.

Hairnets were used to help frame the face. As such, they generally extended from the top of the crown in the back to the nape of the neck. After the war, when hairstyles began to have more height, the top of the hairnet slipped downward on the back of the head until the tops of the hairnets were even with the tops of the ears.

Variations

Fine, dark, hairnets—When hairnets were worn, the single most popular style was a net made of a fine, dark-colored thread netted in a plain, fishnet pattern.

Usage—The absence of a net is more common than the presence of a cap in all age groups. The 15-25 age group appeared in nets nearly half the time, more than any other age group. The vast majority of these nets appear dark, meaning either entirely dark, or dark with light colored beads.

Misconceptions

One widespread misconception about headwear of the Civil War period is that all women wore white hairnets made of a heavy yarn or thread, and that they wore these "snoods" all the time. My research has shown this as being far from a "rule." In fact, the wearing of light colored hairnets by adults was so rare that including one in an impression of the period actually reduces the accuracy of the impression. In addition, the wearing of hairnets of any kind, light or dark, was the exception, rather than the norm.

Common Elements

Nets were not worn by a majority of women. However, when nets were observed, they often had decorative ribbons attached to them which helped to frame the face. Two general types of hairnets were observed:

☞ Those made of a fine thread and woven or "netted" in a plain, fishnet pattern. The holes in these nets were just about large enough to allow a pencil to pass through.
☞ Those made of heavier materials, such as ribbons and heavier yarn. These, too, most often appear to be of plain fishnet patterns.

Key Characteristics

The decorative nets, termed "snoods" in modern sources, were a fad that became popular among young women in the period. Some continued to wear them after the war, so many

Pre-Civil War photographs do not provide much evidence of hairnets.

These two photographs show women wearing a fine net at the back of their head. The hair is confined, and the net is worn over it.

Post-war photographs provide more evidence of mature women wearing hairnets.

Hairstyles of post-Civil War women emphasized height and used a hairnet which slipped down on the back of the head.

Construction Tips—One set of memoirs from the period includes an incident in which hairnets were made by netting thread over a pencil. Undoubtedly, many were netted at home. Fashion magazines sometimes included step-by-step instructions for netting, often assuming that the reader would know what to make from the instructions. For the last 30 years (at least) convincing brown colored nets have been for sale in variety stores where they are sold as a covering for hair curlers.

Instances of possible hairnets (Ribbons)—Since hairnets are worn on the back of the head, and many of the photographs were taken from the front, efforts were made to detect any evidence of a hairnet in the photograph. Thus, the women in photographs who appeared to be wearing the decorative ribbons often attached to hairnets, were counted as wearing hairnets.

Usage—The decorative ribbons sometimes seen on hairnets were observed in the same general age groups as the hairnets themselves: Some in the 15-25, less in the 26-40 age group, with very little evidence in the 41-65 and 66+ age groups.

Construction Tips—The decorative ribbons appear most often to be made of velvet. The ribbon is pleated or twisted so that it has some depth when viewed from the front. This decorative element generally extends from one ear to the other. A reproduction of a ribbon can be made with a flat band hidden inside, which will help the wearer to hold it on her head.

Light colored hairnets—An insignificant minority of young women were observed to have or be wearing hairnets that appeared to be lighter than the color of their hair. Light colored hairnets are most often seen on children.

The two photographs at right show examples of decorative hairnets made of velvet ribbon, mainly worn by women of younger ages.

CAPS

Key Characteristics

Caps of the Civil War period frame the face, adding more width than height.

After the Civil War period, caps were seldom worn, except as costume items, by servants (and by women in conservative religious sects). These post-war caps and hair ornaments are shaped in a manner that adds to the illusion of height, rather than framing the face like Civil War period caps.

Variations

Caps covering the crown of the head—Caps which covered the entire crown of the head, extending from ear to ear (and often tying under the chin) were most often made of white fabric. They were seldom trimmed.

Usage—The absence of a cap is more common than the presence of a cap in all age groups except the 66+ group. In that group, more than 80% were observed wearing caps. The most common style of cap in this 66+ age group is one that was only rarely seen on younger women and was one that covered the entire crown of the

Misconceptions

One popular misconception about headwear of the Civil War period is that all proper women wore something on their heads at all times, indoors and out. My research has illustrated that this statement is *not* true for a majority of women having their photographs made indoors. An unscientific review of photographs taken in military settings also indicates that women did not *always* wear headwear when out of doors.

Common Elements

Caps were not worn by a majority of women. However, when caps were observed, they fell into two classes:

☞ Those worn by women under age 65, which generally covered the back of the head, and served to "frame" the face. These most often appear dark in the photographs, and are usually trimmed in small amounts of slightly gathered lace.

☞ Those worn by women over age 65, which generally covered the entire crown of the head, from ear to ear. These most often appear light, even white, in the photographs, and are seldom trimmed with anything but the fabric itself.

Prior to the Civil War some older women favored a cap which covered the entire crown of the head. They continued wearing this hairstyle both during and after the Civil War.

head, from ear to ear. This type of cap was not observed in any photographs of women who appeared to be younger than 40.

Construction Tips—Patterns and illustrations for constructing a cap of this sort can be found in pre-Civil War sources, like the *Working Woman's Guide* that dates from the 1830s. The cap should be constructed of a tightly woven white cotton fabric, and should be large enough to cover the crown of the head. Many infant's caps of this style exist in antiques shops. If the hair is confined at the back, a cap like this can be secured to the head with straight pins, which are more appropriate, more invisible, and just as effective, as modern bobby pins.

Caps at back of head—Women under age 65 who wore caps in their photographs generally wore ones which covered the back of the head. These caps appear dark in the photographs, and often appear to be trimmed with small amounts of loosely gathered lace. They most often sit on the back of the head, and do not have ties.

Usage—Caps worn on the back of the head were seen most often on women in the 41-65 age group.

Construction Tips—Remember, the lace used in constructing caps of this sort was relatively expensive. A woman might trim her cap in lace, but the body of the cap was likely to be a fine net, rather than a second, or third, different pattern of lace. Several original caps were observed having a fine wire sewn near the edge of the cap

to help it hold its shape. If the hair is confined, caps of this sort can be held on with dark colored straight pins.

Religious caps—An insignificant minority of young and old women were observed to have or be wearing extremely stiff, translucent caps similar to those still worn in some conservative religious communities.

Following the Civil War, the cap was used to emphasize height, rather than width.

In areas where machine-made trims were available, caps were sometimes made with tightly gathered trims.

Women in younger age groups usually preferred not to wear a cap.

Caps were more common on women in older age groups.

Cap covering the crown of the head.

A women wearing a religious cap.

In this photograph, the woman appears to be making a cap.

HAIRSTYLES

Key Characteristics

In the majority of hairstyles, the hair was arranged so that the fullest part of the hairstyle was at or below the ears. Just at the end of the war, and in years thereafter, the hair was arranged to be fullest at or above the temples, and it was arranged with greater height. Bangs on the forehead were virtually unknown among Americans in this period (or were unintentional). However, immediately following the Civil War, some styles became popular that included tendrils on the forehead. Blow dryers had not yet been invented, and as the hair was brushed during the drying process, it was generally trained to lie flat against the scalp, especially at the part.

Variations

Confined (to hairline)—The single most popular style was to part the hair in the center and arrange it so the widest part of the style was at the ears, and the remainder extending down the back of the head to about the hairline.

Misconceptions

One popular misconception about hairstyles of the Civil War period is that they do not matter, and that a reasonably accurate impression of the past can be achieved with accurate clothing, but a modern hairstyle. Hairstyles of the period are so consistent, and so different from modern hairstyles, that a "look" of the period cannot be achieved without a period hairstyle.

Common Elements

Hairstyles in the Civil War period emphasized the width of the face by leaving the forehead bare at the center and being arranged to frame the face with width at the sides but no height at the top. The hair was generally confined. For day wear, women of the period contrived to hide the ends of the individual strands of hair, even when fixing the hair in braids or ringlettes. The exception to this was hairstyles of teens who sometimes still wore their hair blunt cut to a length below the lobes of the ears, in the style so popular for children.

Prior to the Civil War, some older women favored a hairstyle in which curls were worn at the temples. They continued wearing this hairstyle during and after the Civil War.

Following the Civil War, the emphasis of hairstyles was above the ears (during the war it was at or below). This photo is dated July 1866.

Bangs were reintroduced after the war, and remained in use for decades. Photo is dated March 20, 1881.

Usage—"Confined" hairstyles appeared more than any other type of hairstyle. This is true in all age groups. However, the shape of the hairstyle varied by age. Among older women, the hair was confined at the back to about the hairline, while among younger women, it often extended to the nape of the neck.

Construction Tips—To make the hair lie flat on the top, brush it and allow it to dry without the use of a blow dryer. Brush from the top, always downward, with bristle ends aimed at (not away from) the scalp.

If bangs are a problem, start at the part, and try twisting them around themselves, and then twisting in with them the hairs that grow along the hairline, creating a roll that extends along the hairline from the front part to the back of the ears. The roll can be secured behind the ears with a pin.

Unconfined hairstyles—Two variant hairstyles seen on young women were styles in which the hair was parted in the center, then fixed in ringlettes which hang from the crown, and styles in which the hair was parted in the center, but hung loose in a relatively short, blunt, haircut.

Usage—Ringlettes were worn by women in both the 15-25 and 26-40 age groups, but were not seen on women in older age groups (except in post-war pictures). Short hair cuts were seen on a small portion of women in the 15-25 age group. In both cases (ringlettes and short hair), the hair was parted in the center and pulled away from the forehead.

Construction Tips—The ringlettes are tight and narrow. They can be created by separating the hair into even strands, and twisting the hair around itself, or around a very small curling iron while wet with water or stiffener, and allowing the hair to dry while being held in the curl. At the bottom of the ringlette, the ends of the hair should be pushed up inside the ringlette.

If bangs are a problem with a shorter hair style, lift up the hair which grows from the crown of the head, and use mousse or stiffener to secure the bangs off the forehead. When the crown hairs are laid back down, they will conceal the ends of the bangs.

Curls at the temples—A small portion of women in the 66+ age group were observed to have a portion of the hair from the crowns of their heads arranged in ringlettes at the temples. This was a holdover of a style that had been popular in a previous decade, particularly during the 1840s. Other older women sometimes continued to wear their hair in a double part, or a "Y" part, also styles which had been popular in previous decades.

The single most popular hairstyle was confined to the hairline.

The most popular hairstyle among young women was confined to the nape of the neck.

All-over ringlettes.

Short hair was more common in the younger age groups.

Alternate part, mostly seen on older women. (pre-war photo)

ENSEMBLES

Key Characteristics

One key characteristic of Civil War period dresses, in both bodice and skirt combinations, and dresses in which the bodice and skirt were not detachable, was the presence of a waist seam that completely encircled the waist. Exceptions to this were:

☞ Maternity and mourning gowns which sometimes had no waist seam at the front but still had one at the back.

☞ "Empress Eugenie" gowns shaped from fabric pieces that extended from shoulder seam to hem. This style of dress became most popular after the war when dresses with less fullness at the hips became fashionable. There is little evidence of these dresses being worn during the war months; they came into wide use just after the war.

Variations

Single-fabric ensemble (dress)—The single, most common bodice style—for all age groups—was the bodice and skirt made of the same fabric, and worn as a dress.

Misconceptions

One widespread misconception about ensembles of the Civil War period is that women wore outfits of "mix-and-match" separates. Another is that women who wore matching bodices and skirts in their photographic portraits then wore (more fashionable) shirt-and-skirt combinations in less formal situations. This is as logical as believing that women today who have formal portraits made in sundresses change into designer gowns to clean their fishbowls. In reality, most women of the Civil War era had their photographs made while wearing their normal, everyday clothing.

Common Elements

A majority of women in all age groups wore dresses composed of matching bodices and skirts that were attached to each other, or of matching bodices and skirts worn as ensembles. When the bodice had a waistband sewn to it, the skirt waistband was worn outside the bodice waistband. When the bodice did not have a waistband, the bodice was worn outside, concealing the skirt waistband.

Pre-Civil War photographs do not provide much evidence of contrasting bodices and skirts.

Bodices and skirts of different fabrics were not used until after the Civil War.

Post-Civil War "Empress Eugenie" dress without a waist seam.

Matching bodice and skirt ensemble.

Usage—Among the entire population, the single-fabric ensemble of a matching bodice and skirt appeared more than any other type of ensemble. In every age group, it was significantly more common than any other ensemble style. Only in the 15-25 age group did a significant minority of women wear a bodice (or shirt) and skirt of different fabrics.

Construction Tips—Dresses were generally constructed by finishing the bodice and skirt as complete garments, and then basting the two together at the waist. Unmatched bodices and shirts should be used with discretion: One woman submitted her war-time remembrances to *Godey's* magazine. In her (late 1860s) article, she commented that "even now, I cannot see a young lady on the street in her (unmatched) shirt and skirt without thinking to myself 'Poor girl, can't do any better.'"

Unmatched bodices and skirts—When women had their photographs taken in outfits that did not consist of the single-fabric ensemble, the bodice was generally some color other than white.

Usage—The unmatched bodice (or shirt) and skirt was more common in the 15-25 age group than any other age group. Even among this age group, only a small minority wore unmatched bodices and skirts. On these rare occasions, it was more common to see a solid bodice (or shirt) and skirt. The second most common combination was a solid bodice (or shirt) and printed skirt. Rarest of all was the printed bodice and solid skirt. This last variation was so uncommon that it was statistically insignificant. There were, however, instances of print bodices with (different) printed skirts, but these were noted mainly on children. Studies of original garments outside of this study of photographs have turned up little or no evidence that shirts (as opposed to bodices) were ever made of printed fabrics for adults in this period.

Construction Tips—When unmatched bodices and skirts were worn, they appeared to be lined and finished just like other bodices. Each garment is completely finished and the two are then basted together. This basting helps prevent "gap-osis" between the bodice and skirt.

The matching bodice and skirt was worn by all ages.

Unmatched bodice and skirt.

Different fabrics, both solids.

Girl wearing a solid bodice and a print skirt.

BODICES

Common Elements

The most popular bodice style for women of all ages was the shaped or "V" bodice. The gathered or "O" bodice was a popular variation among younger women, while the fan-front or "Y" bodice was a popular variation for older women.

Pre-Civil War bodices are sometimes longer than the natural waistline. The waistlines of Civil War period bodices are located at the natural waistline. In the years just before the war, and during the war, waistlines were cut progressively higher. After the war and in the late 1860s, bodices became shorter, so the waist was above the natural waist line.

Key Characteristics

Key characteristics of bodices of the Civil War period include lines which helped to emphasize the narrowness of the waist and the width of the shoulders:

☞ Shoulder seams were lengthened and armscyes (armhole seams) shaped to appear as diagonal, rather than vertical lines. Armscyes fit closely under the armpit.

☞ The dresses fasten at the center front, but trim (if any) was most often applied in horizontal, rather than vertical lines.

☞ Sleeves were fullest at the elbow, making the waist look small by comparison.

Misconceptions

One common misconception is that women of all ages were equally likely to wear any of the various bodice styles common in the period.

Fitted "V" bodice.

Gathered "O" bodice.

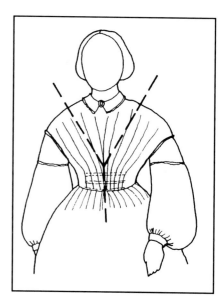

Fan front or "Y" bodice.

Civil War period bodices also had characteristics evident in studying originals (but not in viewing photographs). They include:

☞ Fastening with hooks and eyes (eyes were sewn at fabric's edge, and hooks recessed from the edge about an inch).

☞ (Self-fabric) fine piping sewn in the armscyes.

(Below, left) Bodices fasten at the center-front while skirts have a side-front opening.

(Below) Armscye piping shown on back of bodice.

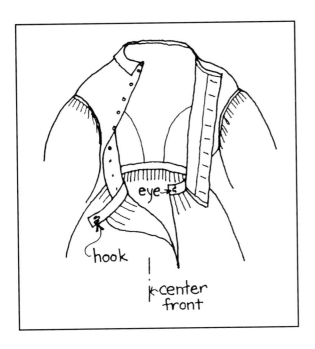

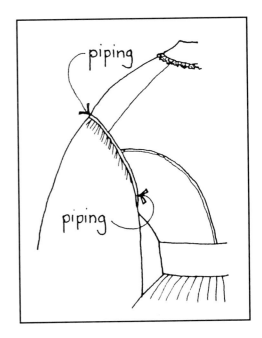

Prior to the Civil War, waistlines sometimes extended below the waist at the front.

Following the Civil War, armscyes were only barely diagonal.

Vertical trim became very popular after the Civil War.

Variations

Fitted or "V" bodices—The single most popular style of bodice for all age groups was the fitted or "V" bodice.

Usage—While the fitted bodice was the most popular bodice in all age groups, it was especially favored among women in the 26-40 and 41-65 age groups.

Construction Tips—"V" bodices were shaped to the body with double (or earlier, triple) vertical darts at the front and with side-back seams that extended in a quarter-circle arc from armscye to within an inch of the center back at the waist. Reproduction dresses often have these seams too far apart at the waist.

Fitted bodices were constructed with linings cut much like the bodice pieces themselves. The fabric and lining pieces were sewn together, and then the bodice constructed. Raw edges were visible on the inside of the garment. Elaborate finishes and featherstitching on these raw edges is a post-war characteristic.

The fitted, or "V" bodice was the most popular bodice among all age groups.

Gathered or "O" bodices—A popular style of bodice, particularly among young women, was a gathered into the waistband with fullness at the front (and presumably the back) but not the sides.

Usage—Gathered bodices appear in significant numbers only in the younger age groups, appearing most among the 15-25 and 26-40 groups. Some of the bodices which appear as gathered bodices are, in fact, shirts.

Construction Tips—A study of original "O" bodices reveals that they most often have underbodices which are shaped like fitted bodices. The gathered fabric lies loosely over the underbodice, attached (most often) only at the shoulders, neck, waist, and side seams.

Gathered or "O" bodice.

Fan-front or "Y" bodices—One style of bodice which was popular before the war, and among older women during the war, was the fan-front, or "Y" bodice. This bodice had dress fabric cut so that it laid in gentle folds over the bosom, and was pleated, gauged, or gathered into the waist at the center front (and presumably, back). These bodices differ from gathered bodices because the fabric is often pleated or gathered at the shoulder, as well as the waist.

Usage—Fan-front and modified fan-front bodices appeared in significant numbers only among women in the 66+ age group. One of the few statistically significant findings of the urban-versus-rural comparison was that this bodice was somewhat more popular in rural areas. However older women in the city favored the bodice far more than young women in rural areas.

Construction Tips—Fan bodices are constructed like "O" bodices except that the dress fabric is pleated, gauged, or gathered only at the center front (and back).

Fan-front, or "Y" bodice.

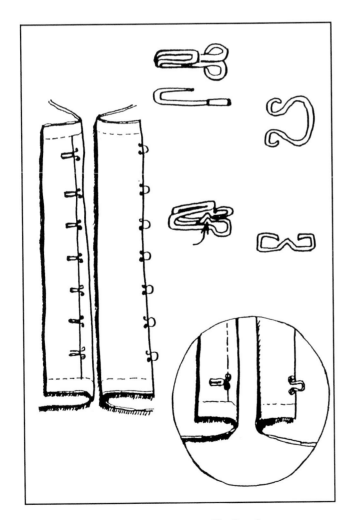

Detail showing placement of bodice fasteners (hook and eyes).

Modified fan-front bodice (note pleats).

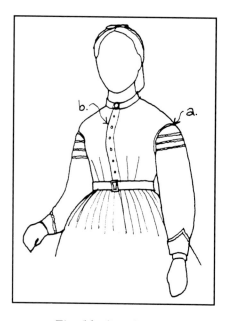

Front of bodice. The most common style of bodice has double vertical darts, a center front fastener, and piping at the neck and armscyes.

Fitted bodice, front
a. armscye
b. center-front opening

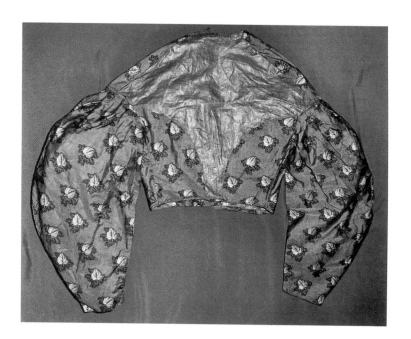

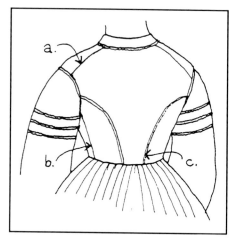

Back of bodice. The center-back piece of this bodice was removed and the fabric presumably reused. The shiny brown lining is left exposed and is typical of many originals.

Fitted bodice, back
a. shoulder seam
b. side seam
c. side-back seam

WHITE SHIRTS

Misconceptions

One common misconception is that women of all ages wore outfits consisting of white shirts and various skirts. Another is that the decision to wear a "waist" or "jacket" was dependent upon the weather.

Common Elements

A very small minority of women in the 15-25 age group sometimes wore ensembles consisting of white shirts and skirts. In photographs taken during the beginning and middle years of the war, they consistently accessorized white shirts with "waists" or "jackets." Only in the last months of the war did many women begin to wear white shirts without jackets or waists.

Key Characteristics

Key characteristics of white shirts for women of the Civil War period are consistent with period bodice construction and styling:

☞ Armscyes well off the shoulder.
☞ Center-front fasteners (even if the fasteners were cleverly hidden).
☞ Sleeves full and large at the elbow.

Civil War period shirts also had the characteristics of:

☞ Fastening with buttons and buttonholes, rather than the hooks and eyes more common on bodices.
☞ Having straight, full sleeves which gathered into a wristband, rather than the two-piece sleeves so common on bodices.
☞ Being sewn into waistbands. They did not have "shirt-tails," like men's shirts or women's shirts of later periods.

Variations

White shirts worn with "waists" or jackets—During the early and middle years of the war, young women who wore white shirts, consistently wore "waists" or jackets over them. A "waist" might be considered the feminine version of a period vest. As is consistent with the "look" of the period, a "waist" had horizontal, rather than vertical, lines.

Usage—The minority of young women who wore white shirts consistently accessorized them with "waists" and jackets. The jackets were of a style similar to that known today as a "bolero." They had a variety of names in the period.

Construction Tips—Jackets were commonly (though not always) the same fabric as the skirt. "Waists" were universally solid fabrics which appear dark and shiny in the photographs.

White shirts without jackets—A minority of women in late-war photographs (taken in the last eight months of the war) wore white shirts without jackets. The number of such photographs in this study was statistically insignificant, however, they do show a transition to a style that increased in popularity after the war.

Usage—The occurrence of white shirts worn without "waists" or jackets was confined to photographs taken in the last eight months of the war. A few fashionable young women in port cities might have adopted this fashion for occasional use in those months before the surrender.

Construction Tips—White shirts worn without "waists" or jackets were made of a sturdy cotton fabric woven tightly enough to be opaque. The lines of chemises and corsets should not be visible through the fabric.

Garibaldi shirts—The distinctive Garibaldi shirt with trim at center front, waistband, shoulders and cuffs, was favored by fashionable young women during and just after the Civil War. Garibaldi shirts for adults were generally made of colored fabrics, white ones being considered *en negligee* for adults.

(Above) Pre-Civil War photos provide little evidence of shirts.

(Above) White shirts worn without "waists" or jackets were common after the Civil War.

(Below, left) Bodices were more common than shirts in all age groups.

(Below) Post-Civil War shirts without full, gathered sleeves.

(Above) White shirt worn with a jacket.

(Above) Shirt worn with a "waist."

(Below, left) Colored shirt worn without a jacket.

(Below) Garibaldi shirt.

NECKLINES

Key Characteristics

Key characteristics of necklines of the Civil War period are that they helped to enhance width in the face. The round collars that were fitted at the base of the neck served this purpose. Necklines which exposed the chest drew attention away from the face, and were not used for day wear. Even when older women wore "V" necklines, they filled in the chest area with chemisettes that had round, "jewel" necklines.

Collars most often followed the lines of the round neckline, and terminated at the front with edges that extended diagonally out from a broach or pin. Older-style lace collars mainly worn by older women were cut so that the edges extended horizontally out from the broach or pin. Collar edges were not generally flush with each other.

Wide necklines which bared the tops of the shoulders, but not the chest were typical prior to the Civil War.

Misconceptions

One common misconception is that women wore the same variety of necklines on their day dresses as those that appear in fashion magazines for semi-formal and formal dresses. Another is that women used collars solely as decorative elements.

Common Elements

A single shaped neckline was far more popular for day dresses than any other. It was the round, "jewel" neckline that fit closely to the base of nape of the neck.

Women wore collars with their dresses as an economical measure. Sewing fabric collars to the inside of the dress helped to protect the neckline against the soils and wear from rubbing against the neck. This helped to prolong the life of the dress, and was consistent with the economics of the era. Collars were basted into (not onto) dresses in order to save dress fabric from wear and tear.

Variations

Round "jewel" neckline—The single most popular style of neckline for all age groups was the round or "jewel" neckline that was fitted to the nape of the neck.

Usage—While the round "jewel" was the most popular neckline in all age groups, it was universally favored by women in the 26-40 and 41-65 age groups. There were very few women in these age groups who used any other neckline.

Construction Tips—The necklines fit closely to the nape of the neck, and there is evidence from original garments that if the neckline was too loose, fabric was pieced in to make it fit properly.

Many of these necklines had piping sewn to their edges. The piping was made of a bias strip of the dress fabric itself which was folded over a fine piece of string. (Fine crochet thread will serve the purpose.)

Wide or "boat" necklines—A relatively small number of women in the 15-25 age group wore dresses with the wide necklines that extended horizontally from the one shoulder bone to the other, baring the tops of the shoulders, but not the chest. This had become a traditional style for children's dresses. Many of these garments also had other child-like characteristics, such as short sleeves and skirts.

Usage—The wide or "boat" neckline was normally used on children's dresses still being worn by teens. It was not commonly found on dresses that were designed for older women.

Construction Tips—Dresses with these wide necklines are sometimes misidentified as evening gowns. The wide neckline is actually higher than those found on evening gowns, and does not dip downward at the center front as evening gowns sometimes did.

"V" necklines with chemisettes—One style of neckline which was popular before the war, and among older women during the war, was the "V" neckline that was often formed where fan-front bodice pieces met in a "V" shape at the chest. Women then wore an undergarment known as a chemisette to cover their chest to the nape of the neck.

Usage—"V" necklines and chemisettes were worn exclusively by women in the 41-65 and 66+ age groups. They were not observed on younger women, even those in conservative and religious clothing.

Construction Tips—Chemisettes were most often side-less, sleeve-less shirts resembling long, wide, front-and-back-dickies. These garments are illustrated in some fashion magazines as tieing at the waist so the front and back pieces did not shift. They are also sometimes illustrated with sleeves.

After the Civil War women wore neckline trim that emphasized the chest.

Necklines with vertical lines which made the neck appear longer were more common in post-Civil War fashion.

Round "jewel" neckline.

Wide neckline worn by children and some teens.

Fabric collar attached to inside of neckline.

Usually, only actresses bared their chests during the day.

"V" neckline worn with chemisette.

COLLARS

Lay-down collars generally extended most of the way around the neck, terminating in straight edges that fell in diagonals (younger women) or horizontal ends (older women). The collar edges seldom met at the front.

Most collars were sewn flat, and the incidents of gathered, pleated, or ruffled collars are rare. These became more popular after the Civil War.

Variations

Collar styles: "lay-down," "stand-up," and chemisette—
The three prominent styles of collars were the rounded collars that lie down on the dress, collars cut of a straight piece of fabric which stood up, and a collar formed on a dickie-like garment known as a "chemisette."

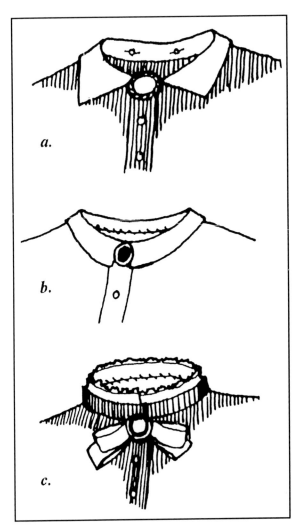

Misconceptions

Common misconceptions about collars of the Civil War period include the idea that most collars were made of lace or crochet work; were often wide; and that "Peter Pan" type collars (which lie down on the dress) were sometimes made of the dress fabric itself.

Common Elements

This study revealed that the majority of collars from the Civil War period were relatively narrow (less than 2.5" wide), and were generally made of white fabric. When dress fabrics were used to make collars, they were generally of the short, stand-up style.

Key Characteristics

Key characteristics of collars in the Civil War period are that they were most frequently sewn to the inside, rather than the outside, of dresses. They were made of white or extremely light-colored fabrics which could withstand frequent laundering. The collars often had little trim on them, and at times only some white-work embroidery or a very narrow edging of lace sewn flat into the edge of the fabric.

Common collar variations
a. lay-down collar with horizontal ends
b. lay-down collar with diagonal ends
c. stand-up collar

Usage—The "lay down" collar was observed on more than 50% of the women in all age groups. The "stand-up" collar was favored by a minority of women in the 15-25 and 26-40 age groups. The chemisette was worn only by a small minority of women, and only in the 41-65 and 66+ age groups.

Construction Tips—Both the "lay-down" and "stand-up" collars were often affixed to dresses with piping at the neckline. Dresses with "V"-shaped necklines seldom had the piping in the neckline.

White fabric collars constructed with narrow tapes sewn to the neckline are easiest to baste to the dress. Fold the tape inside the neckline, and baste the tape to the fabric which forms the neckline facing.

Collar fabrics—The vast majority of collars observed in this study were light colored, and made of fabric rather than lace. Stand-up collars were sometimes made of the dress fabric, and these often had light colored stand-up collars slightly taller than the dress-fabric collar sewn to the inside of the dress.

Usage—White collars were worn by more than three quarters of the women in all age groups. Lace, rather, than fabric, collars, occurred in a small percentage of women in all age groups. Dark collars were worn almost exclusively by women in the older age groups; their frequency increased with the age of the wearer. Only a very small minority in the (15-25) wore dresses with no collar at all.

Construction Tips—Collar fabrics in the Civil War period were generally very practical; cotton fabrics that could be frequently laundered and effectively starched. These cotton fabrics also withstood basting and re-basting without damage.

Width of collars—Research has indicated that the width of necklines was age-dependent, with younger women preferring a more narrow collar.

Usage—More than 75% of girls in the 15-25 age group wore collars that were an inch or less in width. In the 26-40 age group, almost 75% illustrated the same preference. Women in the 41-65 were equally divided on the one-inch collars and those of wider measurements. Only in the 66+ age group did a majority of women prefer collars wider than about an inch.

Construction Tips—When liquid starch is used on collars, the starch does not need to be applied with every laundering; often enough starch remains in the fabric to allow several launderings before needing to be reapplied.

Pre-Civil War collars were wider and had horizontal ends.

After the Civil War, machine-made lace was gathered into neck ruffles.

Taller, stand-up collars that made the neck appear long and trim became common following the Civil War.

Round fabric collars were less than 2.5 inches wide.

Some older women wore wide lace collars.

Narrow collars (often an inch or less wide) were worn by younger women.

Stand-up collars sometimes had inner collars as well.

A dress with no collar at all.

SLEEVES

Misconceptions

Common misconceptions about sleeves are that women of the Civil War period were equally likely to wear any of the various sleeves styles seen during the period.

Common Elements

This study demonstrated that two styles of sleeves were far more popular than any of the several other styles, accounting for approximately 75% of the sleeves observed in every age group. The first of these is the two-piece shaped sleeve which resembles a man's coat sleeve of the period. The second is a straight, full, rectangle gathered into a band or cuff at the wrist.

Sleeves of the period were consistently attached to the bodice with a narrow, self-fabric piping between the sleeve and bodice. In an effort to save fabric, sleeves were often "pieced" together.

Key Characteristics

Key characteristics of sleeves in the Civil War period include the following:

☞ They were shaped with exaggerated fullness at the elbow. This fullness helped to make the waist look smaller by comparison. Sleeves from immediately before and just after the war were narrower at the elbow.

☞ They were attached to the armscye in a manner that provided a relatively smooth line from neck to elbow. This smooth line helped to create an illusion of wide, sloping shoulders. The sleeves were sometimes gathered or pleated into the armscye, but these gathers and pleats did not add fullness at the top of the shoulder. Sleeves were made of the dress fabric; to have a bodice of one fabric and sleeves of another makes the torso and shoulders look more narrow, and these were not desirable features in the period.

Variations

2-piece "coat" sleeve—The 2-piece "coat" sleeve was more popular than any other sleeve style, and continued in popularity—in a narrower variation—even after the Civil War.

Usage—More than 50% of women in the 26-40 and 41-65 age groups favored this sleeve over any other. In the 15-25 age group, and the 66+ age group, only about one-third wore this type of sleeve.

Construction Tips—The sleeve is composed of two pieces. The top piece is cut wider than the bottom piece. Both are shaped so that the edge toward the front is relatively straight, while the back edge is curved outward, particularly at the elbow.

Gathered sleeves—The second-most-popular sleeve was a sleeve cut extremely full at the elbow which was gathered at the wrist into a band or cuff.

Usage—This sleeve was observed on more than 40% of women in the 66+ age group. At the other end of the age spectrum, nearly 30% of women aged 15-25 were observed wearing these sleeves. They were less popular among women in the 26-40 and 41-65 age groups, which preferred the 2-piece "coat" style sleeve.

Construction Tips—A gathered sleeve is generally composed of a single, rectangular, piece of fabric which extends from armscye to wrist. At the wrist, the fabric is gathered into a cuff or band. If the cuff buttons, it does so on the inner (thumb) side of the wrist.

Pagoda sleeves—Full pagoda sleeves become progressively wider to their (usually 3/4 length) hems. Modified pagoda sleeves become only slightly wider to the hem.

Usage—Full and modified pagoda sleeves were most popular among women in the 26-40 and 41-65 age groups, in which nearly 25% were observed wearing them. Only small minorities of women in the 15-25 and 66+ age groups were observed wearing them.

Construction Tips—Because the inside of a pagoda sleeve is often visible, they frequently have wide facings along the inside of the hems. These facings are made of the dress fabric, sometimes decorated with a gathered or pleated line of self-fabric trim on the inside along the facing.

Short sleeves—A small minority of women in the 15-25 age group were observed in short sleeves, a characteristic of children's dresses which some young teens continued to wear as they adopted adult clothing styles.

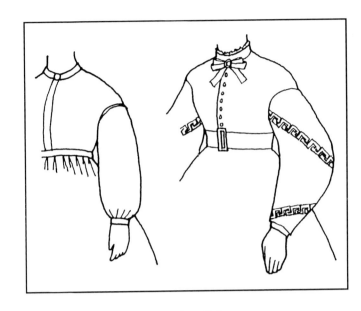

(Left) Gathered sleeve.
(Right) 2-piece coak sleeve.

Narrow sleeves were popular in the 1840s and pagodas in the 1850s.

After the war, sleeves became narrower, especially at the elbow.

Some sleeve styles were popular both during and after the Civil War. (post war photograph)

Sleeve gathered into a band or cuff at the wrist.

Two piece sleeve with exaggerated width at elbow.

Full pagoda sleeve.

Modified pagoda sleeve.

Short sleeves were worn by young teens.

CUFFS AND UNDERSLEEVES

absence of a cuff was easier to determine. In cases where a reliable observation could be made, cuffs were present about 20% of the time. Overall, in photographs where observation was possible, cuffs or undersleeves were apparent more than two-thirds of the time.

Key Characteristics

Key characteristics of cuffs and undersleeves during the Civil War period are that undersleeves were fuller at the elbow than at the wrist. When starched, they served as a foundation garment, helping to maintain the shape of the wide fabric sleeves. They appeared to be trimmed, if at all, with openwork embroidery (known today as eyelet), or with a narrow edging of lace sewn flat to the fabric.

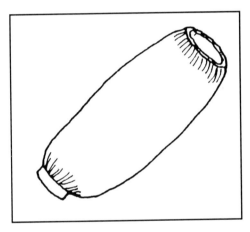

Illustration showing the construction of an undersleeve.

Misconceptions

Separate cuffs and undersleeves are not a part of modern wardrobes, and tend to get overlooked. A popular misconception is that undersleeves were worn only with full or modified pagoda sleeves. This survey indicated that the wearing of undersleeves seemed to be far more universal than as an accessory worn with pagoda sleeves. The use of cuffs and undersleeves seemed to be the rule, rather than the exception.

Common Elements

Detachable cuffs and undersleeves functioned as practical garments, helping to keep the sleeves of the dress clean. As such, they were generally constructed of fine, tightly woven, easily laundered, fabrics.

In many of the photographs, it was difficult to determine the presence or absence of undersleeves. Much of the time, no reliable observation could be made. The undersleeves were observable only when they extended beyond the length of the sleeve, or the arm was positioned so that the undersleeve could be observed on the inside. In the photographs where the presence or absence of an undersleeve could be reliably observed, they were present 96% of the time, and they were present under 2-piece "coat" sleeves, pagoda, modified pagoda, and even the rare tight sleeves. The presence or

Undersleeves were worn under the tight sleeves of the 1840s.

Variations

White or light undersleeves—The vast majority of undersleeves appear to be light or white. Interestingly, there was also a very small number of undersleeves seen with a dark ribbon trim at the wrists.

Usage—In the less than 50% of photographs where reliable observations could be made, nearly all women in the 15-25, 26-40 and 41-65 age groups appeared to wear light or white undersleeves. In the 66+ age group, one in three of those who appeared to be wearing undersleeves wore dark or black, rather than light or white, undersleeves.

Construction Tips—The sleeve is composed of a tube of fabric which ties around the upper arm with a drawstring of narrow, flat, tape (which is more comfortable than string or heavy thread). The undersleeve does not hang loose at the wrist. Rather the overwhelming majority were confined at the wrist by being gathered into (most often) a narrow band. One variation on the undersleeve observed in original garments (but not in photographs) are lacy undersleeves basted to the armscye of the dress. These hang loose at the wrist and could be later additions.

Cuffs—Light or white fabric cuffs were often attached to the inside of the sleeve, then folded back on the outside of the sleeve.

Usage—In photographs where observation was possible, contrasting and presumably detachable cuffs were observed about 20% of the time. This was relatively consistent across all the age groups. Older women, who favored the straight sleeves gathered in at a (self-fabric) cuff, had more cuffs overall, but these non-detachable, self-fabric cuffs were not considered as a part of the survey.

Construction Tips—The detachable cuffs may be constructed double their desired width, sewn to the inside of the sleeve, then doubled back on themselves, folding the edge of the sleeve in between the two parts of the cuff. Cuffs lie better if they are starched. If the cuffs are to button or otherwise fasten, they should do so on the thumb side of the hand.

Undersleeves were also worn under the pagoda sleeves of the 1850s.

Undersleeves continued to be used after the war, white cuffs did not.

Undersleeves were worn under all styles of sleeves.

Undersleeve under a full pagoda sleeve.

White cuffs were sometimes worn instead of undersleeves.

Undersleeve under a modified pagoda sleeve.

White cuffs folded back over the dress sleeve.

GLOVES AND MITTS

Key Characteristics

Key characteristics of gloves and mitts of the Civil War period are that they generally extend only to the wrist, helping to make the hands appear plump, which was a desirable characteristic of the period. Prior to the war years, lace mitts had been fashionable, but these had largely fallen from use (except by older women) during the Civil War. The glove-making industry was a well-developed one by the Civil War period, and women's gloves were manufactured and sold in a wide variety of leathers, sometimes dyed in rather striking colors. Evidence of the manufacturers of these colors can be found in fashion plate descriptions. Evidence of their use in a given area of America is harder to find. Stories of women who wore kid gloves every waking minute of their lives, indoor and out, are largely fictional, and are not reflected in the photographic evidence.

Misconceptions

One widespread misconception about gloves and (especially) mitts of the period is that they were universally worn, and that whether they were worn, or the style that was worn, was a function of the time of day.

Common Elements

Gloves and mitts were not universally worn by women of the Civil War period, either in their studio photographs, or in the photographs of them in less formal situations. When gloves and mitts were observed, they were generally seen in the following situations and styles:

☞ Women wearing bonnets (as to go out of doors) were sometimes photographed in gloves that appeared to be made of tight-fitting kid or leather. These gloves were relatively short, extending only to or just beyond the wrist bone.

☞ Women over age 66+ were occasionally photographed wearing mitts or gloves made of a material that appears in (black and white) photographs to be fine, dark, lace. These may extend to the wrist bone, or more rarely, several inches beyond it.

Mitts were very fashionable in the 1850s.

Variations

Gloves—The vast majority of gloves seen in the photographs appear to be a solid fabric or leather, rather than a crocheted or knitted material.

Gloves were a fashion item, and each season's new styles were published in fashion magazines. In the 1860s gloves often had decorative stitching on the back of the hand. Contemporary evidence indicates that gloves came in a variety of colors including yellow, blue, green, pink, and shades of gray.

Usage—Slightly more than 10% percent of women in the 66+ age group appear to be wearing gloves or mitts. (The statistics for the two were combined in this study.) In the 15-25 age group, only 1%, and in the 26-40 age group, only 2%, wore them. Even in the 41-65 age group, this figure was only 7%. Thus, a small minority of older women wore gloves and mitts, while the number of younger women who did so was very small.

Construction Tips—The gloves observed in photographs were more like the kid gloves worn for church in the first half of the 20th century than the lace and crocheted gloves worn for formal wear in the latter half of the 20th century. In the Civil War period, these generally terminated at or just above the wrist bone.

Mitts—The mitts observed in this study appeared to be made of a fine, dark, lace or net fabric. Heavy thread crochet- or knit-work mitts were not represented. No mitts with beadwork were observed.

Usage—The frequency with which mitts were observed in photographs increased with the age of the wearer, but was a small minority even in the oldest age group.

Construction Tips—The ideal of beauty in the Civil War period dictated that hands and fingers appear plump. Thus, mitts were cut straight across at both ends. There is no evidence for mitts which terminated in a point over the middle finger. A convincing reproduction of mitts of the period can more easily be made of lace or net fabric than of crocheted or knitted yarn.

Mitts continued to be used by some long after the war.

The majority of women, regardless of their age, did not wear mitts or gloves.

Short gloves worn with outerwear.

A good example of lace gloves.

(Below) two photos showing other styles of gloves.

WAIST SHAPES

Variations

Straight waist—The vast majority of waistlines seen in the photographs were straight and were located at the natural waist.

Usage—More than 80% of women in all age groups appeared to have straight waists. In the 66+ age group, this was increased to nearly 90%. However, there was a significant minority of women in that age group posed with their arms in a position that hid their waistlines from view.

Construction Tips—The majority of dresses had bodices which extended over the skirt. When the skirt waistband is secured at the natural waist, the bodice should be long enough to extend to the bottom of the waistband. In this way, there will be no "gapping" between bodice and skirt. This does not work if the waistband is loose or insecurely fastened.

In pre-Civil War fashion the waist extended below the natural waistline at the front.

Misconceptions

One common misconception is that women of all ages were equally likely to wear any of the various waist shapes of the period.

Common Elements

The most popular waist shape of the period was the straight waist, which was observed in more than 80% of the women in all age groups.

Key Characteristics

A key characteristic of waist shapes of the Civil War period are that they appear at the natural waistline. In the period before the Civil War, waists had often been longer, extending below the waist at the center front (and sometimes the back). In the period immediately after the Civil War, waistlines became somewhat shorter, so that even the bottom of a waistband was actually situated above the natural waistline.

Points—Some bodices were observed to have a single or double point at the front. These styles were worn with fitted, "V" bodices. The points appear to be boned so that they lie flat over the skirt.

Usage—Nearly 20% of women in the 26-40 age group favored styles with single or double points. Approximately that many favored them in the 15-25 and 41-65 age groups. None were observed in the 66+ age groups.

Construction Tips—The points will lie flat over the skirt only if the rest of the waist is cut along the waistline of the skirt. The points will lie best if they are boned their entire length, and into the bodice.

Lower waist—About 10% of the women in the 66+ age group (of those where an observation could be made) were observed to have waistlines that dipped downward at the front, like those which had been popular a decade before the war.

(Top, right) Decades after the war, as bodices became longer, the waistline returned to the natural waist.

(Bottom, right) Most women, regardless of age, wore garments with straight waists.

In fashions immediately following the Civil War the waistline is above the natural waist.

The waist was located at the natural waistline.

Bodice with a double point.

Bodice with a single point.

Bodice which dips below the natural waist at the front.

BELTS

Belts were not as popular before or after the Civil War as they were during the Civil War. Thus the use of belts is a key characteristic of the period. Unfortunately, many original garments are displayed in museums without belts, and so an idea of the prevalence of belts can best be seen through a study of photographs.

Variations

Shape of Belts—The vast majority of belts seen in the photographs were straight, many with decorative elements at the front.

Usage—More than 80% of women in the 15-25 age group appeared to be wearing belts. Only in this young age group did a significant portion wear belts with points. In the other age groups, belts were universally straight. The likelihood of a woman wearing a belt decreased with her age.

Construction Tips—The few original belts available for examination fastened with hooks and eyes, having buckles which were purely decorative. The "Medici" belts which are shaped into a point or points at the front (and sometimes the back) generally appear to fasten somewhere other than the center front.

Fabric of belts—The vast majority of belts which were observed appeared to be dark in color, and constructed of solid fabrics.

Usage—The vast majority of belts which contrasted with the fabric of the dresses in the survey appeared darker than the dress fabric. These belts were seen on more than 50% of the members of the 15-25 age group. They were seen in decreasing percentages as the ages increased.

Belts and visible waistbands made of the same fabric as the dresses were more popular among girls in the 15-25 age group. These accounted for nearly 25% of the women in that age group. Dress fabric belts and visible waistbands were visible in decreasing percentages from 25% among those 15-25 to 4% among women 66+ years of age.

Belts of a lighter contrast to the dress were seen on only a few women in the 15-25 age group. None of the older age groups gave any representation of this style.

Construction Tips—The belts seen in the photographs generally appear to be fabric-covered, although some may be leather. Few, if any, of the belts in the photographs appeared to be velvet, and none appeared to have any evidence of lace trim. Only one—a pointed "Medici" belt worn by a young teen—appeared to be beaded.

Misconceptions

One common misconception is that women of all ages were equally likely to wear belts, and were equally likely to wear any of the various styles of belts.

Common Elements

Approximately 50% of the entire population in this study appear to be wearing belts. Of these, the most popular belt was the straight belt, with or without an apparent buckle or fastener.

Key Characteristics

Some key characteristics of belts in the Civil War are that they enhance the overall lines of the garments, placing the emphasis at the center of the waist. Many of the belts had buckles or other decorative devices at the center front. Belts helped to make the waist look more narrow; most appear dark in color, and many contrasted with the fabric of the dress by appearing darker in color than the dress itself. The use of contrasting belts may have been an economic factor, as it permitted a single belt to be worn with any number of dresses.

There is little evidence of the use of belts prior to the Civil War.

During the war only about half of the women appear to be wearing belts.

Belts again passed out of widespread use after the Civil War.

Many of the belts had decorative elements at the front.

Among the women who wore belts, the straight belt was most common.

Many belts contrasted with the dress fabric.

Belts shaped with points are today called "Medici" belts.

This bodice survives with a matching belt. The belt fastens with hooks and eyes. The rosette is made of strips of fabric cut on the bias, floded lengthwise, and pleated in concentric circles.

WAIST TREATMENTS FOR SKIRTS

Key Characteristics

Key characteristics of skirts in the Civil War are that they do not have a wide, flat area at the front of the skirt. It was fashionable during nearly all of the Civil War period to have full, healthy hips. In the last few months of the Civil War, silhouettes changed a great deal, and it became more fashionable to have slender hips. Accordingly, box pleats became far more popular than they had been. These pleats provide a flatter appearance at the hips. In addition, the fullness of skirts began shifting to the back with the widespread adoption of elliptical hoops. One of the features adopted with this fashion change was a redistribution of the pleats in the skirt to provide a flattened area at the center front. This is a change which could be adopted without massive restructuring of the dress, and many, many Civil War period skirts were altered in this manner.

Misconceptions

One common misconception is that women were equally likely to use gathers, gauging (known today as cartridge pleating), directional knife pleats, or box pleats to fasten their skirts to the waistband. Another is that when directional pleats were used, they continued in the same direction all the way around the skirt.

Common Elements

Approximately 50% of the photographs were clear enough to determine the manner in which the skirt was attached to the waistband. This is particularly difficult to determine in the photographs of older women because they were often posed with an arm in front of the waist, and because they were sometimes wearing shawls and other garments that hid the waist from view. In those photographs where the evidence was visible, 80% in all age groups had directional (knife) pleats. Of these, the vast majority clearly changed direction at the center front, which meant that the pleats began with an inverted box pleat at the center front. The two center pleats met at the center front, forming an in inverted "V" shape at the waist. Each successive pleat lay on top of the one closer to the center front, so that the skirt fell in folds which extended downward and outward from the center front of the waist.

Pre-Civil War photographs show bell-shaped skirts which were equally full all the way around the skirt.

Variations

Directional Pleating—The vast majority of skirts seem to be pleated in directional pleats toward the center front of the dress.

Usage—In the 50% of photographs where the waist treatment could be determined, approximately 80% of those in all age groups had directional pleats. The percentage of these pleats that did not change direction at the center front was very low. The 15-25 age group had the largest (but still insignificant) percentage of directional pleats that did not change direction at the center front.

Construction Tips—Studies of original garments, and of side-view photographs, confirm that the directional pleats changed direction again at the sides, forming a box pleat at each side, and at the center back there was generally another inverted box pleat. The pleats hang best if the fabric is turned under at the top before the pleats are created.

Box pleats—Less than 20% of women had box pleats (pleats in which every other pleat facing its predecessor).

Usage—The largest occurrence of box pleats occurred among the 66+ group, in which 20% of those which could be seen appeared to have box pleats; the smallest percentage of these occurred in the 15-25 age group. In all groups, box pleats occurred in only a minority of cases.

Construction Tips—Box pleats can be made to take up more fabric if two box pleats are placed immediately on top of each other. This is constructed by creating two left pleats, one immediately on top of the other, followed by two right pleats, one immediately on top of the other. The pleats lie better if the fabric is folded over before the pleats are created.

Additional waist treatments observed in the study of original garments, but not in the study of photographs, include gauging or cartridge pleating. This is done with several lines of gathering threads run in parallel formation through the fabric, and as the fabric is drawn up into a series of tiny and tight pleats, they sit perpendicular to the outside of the garment. Also observed in originals, but not observable in photographs, is the use of gathering (occasionally seen on work garments made of course fabric), and on dresses remade as costumes.

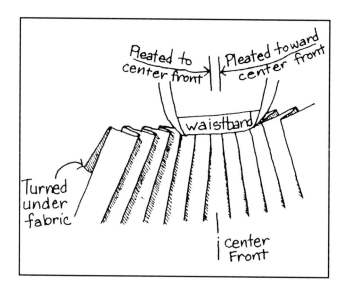

Directional pleating.

Double box pleating.

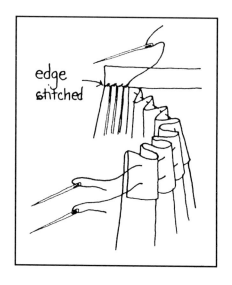

(Right) Cartridge pleating.

In post-Civil War America, box pleats became popular, and progressively larger and flatter.

Pleats were redistributed to provide a flat area at the front of the skirt in the years following the Civil War.

In about half of the photographs the waist treatment can't be seen.

Two-directional pleating was the most common treatment observed.

(Above) Although it appears that the waistline was gathered, it is not possible to determine the exact waist treatment.

(Top, right) An insignificant minority had unidirectional pleats.

(Right) Box pleats.

SKIRT LENGTHS

Misconceptions

One common misconception is that wearing a long skirt (longer than modern day) necessarily means wearing a skirt that touches the ground. Another is that the oft-cited aversion to showing the ankles was still in force during the Civil War.

Common Elements

The vast majority of photographs of women of all ages indicated that skirts did not touch the ground, but were less than 4" off the ground. This practical length prevented the hems from fraying too swiftly, and also reduced the extent to which the skirt from acting as a sponge, mop, and broom.

Key Characteristics

Hemlines were one of the characteristics of clothing (like bonnets) with which women demonstrated how well they kept up with fashion. Fashionable women followed every whim of *Godey's*, lowering their hems to the ground in the 1850s when a glimpse of ankle was supposed to make strong men swoon. These fashionable women raised their skirts by the time of the Civil War to let those men see the clockwork on their stock-

ings, and their horizontally striped stockings. Practical women seemed to always take the middle road. The studio and informal photographs in this study indicated that most women wore their skirts off the ground, but less than 4" off the ground.

Exceptions to this included women who adopted the elaborate elliptical skirt so fashionable just at the end of the war. These skirts were short in the front, but often dragged the ground at the back. After the war, skirts became shorter, to be followed by several decades of elevator-like skirt lengths.

Variations

Up to 4" off the ground—The vast majority of skirts were hemmed so that they did not touch the ground, but were less than 4" off the ground.

Usage—100% of the women in age 66+ group in which the hem could be seen wore their skirts hemmed less than 4" off the ground. This percentage went down as the age decreased, and only slightly more than half (63%) of the women in the 15-25 age group wore their skirts this length.

Construction Tips—Studies of original garments, and trial-and-error with reproductions, confirms that skirts should be hemmed evenly around, and the length of the skirt adjusted at the top before the fabric is turned down and pleated into the waistband.

Hemmed to the floor—Less than 20% of women had their skirts hemmed at the floor.

Usage—The largest occurrence (20%) of floor-length skirts occurred among the 15-25 age group. In the 26-40 and 41-65 age groups, this percentage was closer to 15%. In the 66+ age group, none were observed to have floor-length skirts.

Construction Tips—In order to prevent the edge of the skirt from becoming soiled and frayed, it was often enveloped (after hemming) in a hem protector braid, a 1/2 to 1 inch flat braid of fabric which was stitched on for easy removal. These hem protectors were also sewn on some dresses that were not floor-length. (In an age before the invention of the lawn mower, shorter skirts were also at risk for fraying.)

4" or more off the ground—Additional hem lengths included those that were shorter than 4" off the ground. These were seen (only) in the 15-25 age group, and generally only on women wearing dresses with other childlike characteristics such as short sleeves and wide "boat" necklines.

(Above) Pre-war skirts often touched the floor.
(Below) War-period skirts were less than 4" off the ground.

(Above) Some post-war skirts extended into a slight train.
(Below) Other post-war skirts were hemmed off the ground.

(Top, left) Elderly women universally wore their skirts off the ground.

(Above) Some young teens wore skirts shorter than 4″ off the ground.

(Left) The vast majority of women's skirts did not touch the ground.

PART

3

WHAT WAS WORN

FABRIC

Textures

The fibers used to make fabrics in the nineteenth century included cotton, linen, wool, and silk. Of these, cotton was the least expensive, and silk the most expensive. These four available fibers were spun into thread and woven together in a nearly infinite variety of weights and weaves. After the weaving, any of a number of finishes might be used to further vary the final appearance of the fabric. By the time of the Civil War, the textile industry was extremely well developed, and commercially-produced fabrics were available in even the most remote communities. The shortages caused by the blockade and the war's interruption in trade changed this in some areas during the war. In many cases, the modern textile industry does not produce fabrics in the same weave, and weight, and finish, particularly among the minority of fabrics manufactured today using the original four fibers.

1. (Right) Dresses of extremely valuable fabrics, like this watermark taffeta often had untrimmed skirts, so that the beautiful fabric was not obscured.

2. Fabrics with a shiny texture might be silk, or other fibers with a special finish, much like the chintzes and polished cottons produced today.

3. One popular product of textile mills was fabric with a textured print; a design created not with color, but with variations in the weave.

4. Fabrics with a shiny thread in one direction and a dull thread in another (like silk-wool combinations) had a distinctive texture.

Prints

Even before the introduction of chemical dyes at the end of the 1850s, the textile industry was capable of manufacturing cloth with infinite shades and hues of color.

1. (Left) The 1850s had been a decade of bright colors and relatively large prints. Things toned down a bit in the 1860s, but women were still wearing bright colors, and patterned fabrics. Quilts from the period are excellent sources of information for viewing the colors and color combinations in fabrics of the period.

2. (Right) The photographs indicate that solid fabrics were used more than any other single patterns. Geometric prints were very popular, since they permitted the fabric to be turned upside down when reused.

3. Small geometric prints were the most economical of prints, since little fabric was wasted when matching prints. Originals show evidence of matching prints as small as 1/4 inch checks.

4. Conversely, extremely large prints, especially in silk fabrics, were a sign of wealth.

5. Other popular prints included abstract or floral designs on backgrounds. These designs are often separated from each other by an area the size of the design itself.

TRIM

Materials Used

1. A significant portion of the photographs show women in dresses without any visible trim. (However, these trimless dresses are seldom selected to illustrate books).

2. Some dresses were trimmed with narrow pieces of braid, which were sewn to the dress in intricate, scroll-work patterns. Period sewing machines were sometimes equipped with attachments that made this braidwork easier to complete.

5. The most common material used for trim was either the dress fabric itself, or a contrasting fabric. Often, silk material used for trim was pinked with scallop-shaped punches to make a decorative edge that did not have to be hemmed.

3 & 4. Other popular trims included ribbons and buttons, both of which could be removed and reused when necessary.

Placement

1. (Below) When trim is present, it follows and enhances the desirable lines of the dress. As such, trim on the sleeves helps to emphasize width; horizontal elements at the caps and cuffs help to make the sleeves appear even wider.

2. (Above) Only the most elaborately trimmed dresses had trim on the skirt. There were no examples found of dresses with trim on the skirt and not the bodice.

3. (Left) When skirts were trimmed, the trim was generally horizontal, and placed relatively close to the hem of the skirt. The effect of this trim was to emphasize the fullness of the skirt.

4. (Right) Where trim was visible on many of the dresses, it appeared most on bodices and sleeves, not on skirts.

SPECIAL OCCASIONS

Evening Gowns

Women seldom had their portraits made in evening dress for the obvious reason that photographic techniques required natural sunlight, and evening dresses were not generally worn during the day. Therefore, any photograph of a woman in the period wearing evening dress is by definition an aberration.

Evening dresses were relatively similar to day dresses with the exception that necklines were wide (but still high enough to hide any cleavage), and sleeves were short. Expense was shown in the fine fabrics which were used, and bodices were more commonly trimmed than skirts.

1. Evening hair styles were somewhat less confined than those of day time, and lithographs of women in evening dress show them with curls and tendrils more often than visual images of women in day dress from this period.

2. This woman was photographed with her ermine, as well as her evening gown. The side view shows that the dress is longer at the sides and back than at the front.

3. The teen in this photograph is young enough to wear a day dress with a wide neckline and short sleeves, but the fabrics of this dress are so expensive, that it is undoubtedly for semi-formal or formal wear.

Maternity Dress

For many women of the nineteenth cerntury, being pregnant, or recently pregnant, was a near-constant state. It is not surprising, therefore, that many original garments have evidence of being used for women in this state. Modern Americans are often surprised that obviously pregnant women had studio portraits made. However, diaries and memoirs indicate the fact that being pregnant did not necessarily curtail day-to-day activities.

Maternity clothing followed the same basic styles as other dresses of the period, with bodice-and-skirt combinations of the same fabric. Allowances were made for growth in the stomach with bodices that had drawstrings at the front of the waist. Some such gowns were sometimes made without waist seams in the front, but in this period, even maternity dresses generally had waistseams at the back.

1. This woman, in conservative dress, appears to be in the final weeks of her pregnancy.

2. This woman appears to have quilted front panels in her gown.

3. Some women allowed the waistlines of their dresses to rest on the top of their stomachs, making the dresses appear to have high waists.

4. The design of this coat makes it impossible to tell if the wearer is truly pregnant.

Mourning Dress

In the culture of the nineteenth century, grief at the death of a loved one was displayed in clothing, as well as behavior. Etiquette books of the day contain elaborate rituals for periods of mourning. The extent to which American women followed the rituals was a question of economics, age, and inclination. Photographs probably do not accurately reflect the extent to which mourning dress was worn, since many women did not sit for studio portraits while in mourning.

1 & 2. (Right) Generally, women who dressed for mourning did so by adopting black clothing to include (at least in the initial stages), black collars, cuffs, and/or undersleeves, and black crepe used as veiling, drapes, or trim on otherwise plain dresses.

3. In later stages of mourning, women might indicate their state through changes in behavior (like resuming social roles), and their dress, (as in the use of shiny fabrics, gold jewelry, and white handkerchiefs with black borders).

4. Dark (presumably black, in this case) clothes are not a fool-proof sign that the individual is in mourning, however the black collar and cuffs lend credence to the theory that this woman is in mourning.

Wedding Dress

Although white wedding dresses had come into use by the Civil War period, many women married in one of their better dresses. Thus, any sampling of wedding dresses, or wedding photographs, is likely to be inaccurate; many dresses and photographs which show wedding clothing are simply not identified as such.

However, even when women could afford special clothing for the occassion, they generally wore relatively plain gowns which exhibited their finery in the quality of the fabric rather than the amount of trim.

1. Wedding dresses followed the styles of the period in every way. Weddings were most often held during the day, and wedding dresses were day dresses, with jewel necklines, and long sleeves.

2. It was fashionable for wedding attendants to dress just like the bride, leading to a misidentification of some photographs as "double weddings."

3 & 4. (Above, left & right) In this period where wide faces were fashionable, veils (like hairstyles) provided no height. They lay flat on the top of the head. Headdresses were likely to be coronets of real or artificial flowers which framed the face at the sides as well as the top.

5. (Right) In post-war periods, the headdresses and veils provided height, rather than width.

Furs

In colder weather, and colder climates, fur was used extensively in many forms. Fur was a natural by-product of food production, and was available in both urban and rural areas. Therefore, "high" fashion specified the use of fur types not readily available to the masses.

1. (Right) Ermine had been a fashion fur for several decades prior to the war. Fashion magazines advised that women who could not afford the real thing, could obtain a convincing substitute made from white and dark rabbit fur.

2. (Left) The muffs which appear in Civil War period photographs are fur; later photographs show muffs made of velvet and other fabrics. They were sometimes trimmed with tassels, as this one is. Muffs were effective at keeping the hands warm, but did not help the wrists and arms.

3 & 4. Fur cuffs were sometimes attached to coats or, (apparently) worn as seperate accessories with cloaks.

5. In an era when most conveyances were unheated, fur pieces were often designed for the warmth of the seated figure. They were short, cape-like garments at the back, but long, in the front to cover the entire lap. In open sleighs and carriages, lap robes of heavy furs or fabrics were sometimes used for the same purpose.

Knitted Materials

Knitting and crocheting were skills that most women were expected to acquire. Among the garments women would make with these skills are shawls, scarves, socks, and various undergarments. However, knitted woolen undergarments were perhaps the most common.

1 & 2. (Left & right) Fashion magazines contained patterns and instructions for knitting patterns with color and texture. In one diary, a southern girl comments that the women in the community competed with each other to create the boldest borders on their knitted shawls.

3. Jackets and outerwear were relatively plain, but were sometimes worn with fur or knitted accessories like hoods and scarves. However, for women's wear, hoods seem to have been more common than long scarves, like this one.

4. Women commented in their diaries about spending every spare moment in constructive activities, like knitting. This was especially true during the war, when the need for socks seemed to be neverending. This woman appears to be wearing knitted socks or slippers on her feet.

5. Fashion magazines contained patterns for wrap-around garments like this one, calling them by various names. The garment is constructed of a nearly-rectangular piece with long ends that wrapped around the body, crossing over, and tying over the rectangular piece. Photographs show that the rectangular piece was worn at the front or back.

UNDERGARMENTS

Undergarments served several purposes: Garments such as corsets, crinolines, and corded petticoats gave structure and foundation to women's skirts. Garments like chemises, drawers, under-petticoats, and stockings provided protection for the fine dress fabrics.

Structural Undergarments

Corsets

The use of corsets and the design of garments made the waist look small, especially in comparison to the shoulders, sleeves, and hips. All these things contribute to a myth that "they were all so tiny then." (Photographic evidence refutes this, and many other, sweeping generalizations.)

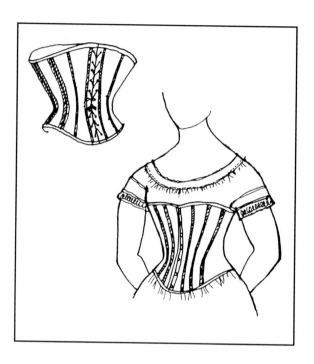

1. The evidence of a corset is sometimes quite obvious, as is evident from the smooth line between the fullest part of the bust and the waist, and by the exceptional fitting of some bodices. This was practical only when the torso could be molded into exactly the same shape and size from one day to another, a feat possible with a corset.

2. The absence of a corset is equally obvious in some photographs, belying the myth that "all women always wore corsets." This woman even posed for a portrait without wearing corsets.

Crinolines and Corded petticoats

One of the most prominent features of clothing in the Civil War period is the size and shape of the skirt. These features are determined in part by the crinolines and corded petticoats worn under the shirt. These undergarments consisted of hoops of stiff materials inserted or woven into petticoat-like garments that held the skirt shape without requiring the wearing of multiple heavy, cumbersome petticoats.

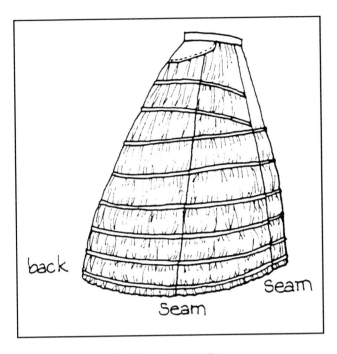

1. Covered crinoline.

2. (Left) Cage crinolines, a variation of the crinoline, consisted of hoops suspended from vertical tapes, much like venetian blinds (or bird cages).

Desired Results in Skirts

The size and shape of skirts are determined by a combination of the skirt and the structural undergarment. The photographs indicate that throughout the war, most women were wearing skirts cut of relatively straight panels and pleated all the way to the center front. These skirts might be worn over a newly-purchased elliptically-shaped crinoline, but would not produce the elliptical silhouette which became fashionable in the second half of the war. This rather exaggerated silhouette did not become a reality for most women until the last month of the war, and for many, until after the war, when they acquired skirts cut as well as pleated to provide a truly flat-fronted silhouette.

Photographs generally show skirt widths that appear to be about 50% as wide as the wearer's heigth. Late-war elliptical-shaped skirts, with their slight trains, appear to be as much as 70% as wide as the height of the wearer.

1. Skirt size.
  a. Height
  b. Skirt is 50% apparent height
  c. Skirt is 70% apparent height

2 & 3. The exaggerated bell shape that appeared in this British caricature (above, left) was modified in real life (above, right).

4. Bell-shaped versus pagoda-shaped skirts. The widest part of a bell-shaped skirt is higher than the more common pogoda-shaped skirt.

5 & 6. The most common skirt shapes in the Civil War period were pagodas, rather than bells. Often, the line of the bottom hoop can be seen about a foot from the ground.

7. The widest skirts of the period were the elliptical skirts that came into use toward the end of the war. These skirts were longer at the back than the front, even dragging on the ground in some photographs.

Protective Undergarments

Chemises, Drawers, and Stockings

Chemises are short-sleeved, loose, shift-like garments. They often had gussets at the armhole to help absorb perspiration and typically required regular laundering. Inventory, laundry, and trousseau lists indicate that women had several, often more chemises than dresses.

1. An original chemise of typical design, gathered into bands at the top.

2. Yoked chemise.

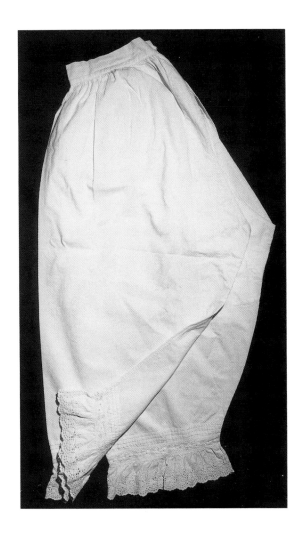

In the first decades of the 19th century, calf- and ankle-length drawers were reintroduced as undergarments for women and girls. These garments typically consisted of two legs independently attached to a waistband. By the time of the Civil War, they extending to just below the knees. In this period, the bottoms of the legs were sometimes decorated with flat tucks, or openwork embroidery sewn relatively flat to the hem.

3 & 4. Drawers were worn by both women and young girls. Those worn by younger and more fashionable women were shorter than the mid-calf-length drawers worn by older and more conservative women.

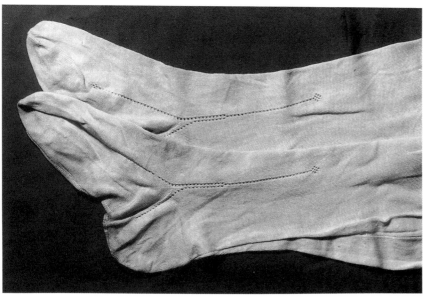

5. A Civil War period CDV of a woman wearing *only* her undergarments is a rarity. However, this photograph provides us with a Parisian illustration of the typical style of undergarments worn by women in the 19th century.

6. Stockings, such as these, were often decorated with various "clockwork" designs. They were generally thigh-high and often knitted of wool, but fashionable women sometimes wore silk stockings. Colored stockings (sometimes with horizontal stripes) were also fashionable in this period.

OUTER WEAR

Women's outerwear of the Civil War period included a number of variations on the basic styles of capes, cloaks, and coats.

Capes

For the purpose of this discussion, a cape is a loose-fitting garment which does not have sleeves, may have arm slits, and is as long on the sides as it is at the front.

1. Capes followed the lines of the garment; cape pieces were cut to lay smoothly over the neck and shoulders. Photographs do not provide evidence for capes which were gathered at the neck, as this was inconsistent with the ideal of sloping shoulders.

2. The capes were generally cut full enough to drape over the dress, and varied in length from hip-length to 7/8 the length of the dress. There is less evidence for capes which extended to the hem of the dress.

3. Generally, capes were made of solid fabrics. They were seldom made of the same fabric as the dress, a style popular earlier in the century.

4. Capes could have arm slits.

Cloaks

For the purpose of this discussion, a cloak is an outerwear garment which has no sleeves, but is constructed to provide for full movement of the arms.

After the war, beaded trim and beaded fringe became extremely popular for both cloaks and coats.

1 & 2. The style of cloaks closely paralleled the lines of dresses; in the Civil War period, they were cut to hang smoothly over sloping shoulders. The body and the arms of the garment were full enough to accomodate the full skirts and sleeves of the period.

3. Cloaks of silk and other fine fabrics were often trimmed with the fabric itself.

4. Fringes were sometimes sewn to fashionable garments.

Coats and Jackets

For the purpose of this discussion, a coat is a garment for outdoor wear which has sleeves on it. The photographs show coats of several lengths being worn in the Civil War period.

Coats of this period followed the lines of other garments. Shoulders sloped downward, sleeves were cut large at the elbow, and the body was wide enough to drape over the large, full skirts.

1 & 2. Short coats and hip length jackets were popular in the period. Some were made of relatively thin fabrics (above, left). Others were lined and made of heavier, woolen, fabrics (above, right).

3 & 4. Other coats were longer, but there is little evidence for coats that were as long as the dresses. Often they were 7/8 the length of the dress, or were hemmed about six inches shorter than the dresses. Many coats appear to have been made of wool.

5. Some coats had fashion features like the exaggerated sleeves of this coat.

Shawls and scarves

Although fashion magazines reported that scarves had gone out of favor, they remained in use for some time. Shawls, however, were ever popular.

1. (Right) Shawls were sometimes made from squares of fabric. Others were full squares of fabric, or even double squares. Paisley shawls, the subject of much literature about the Civil War period, are not commonly seen in photographs. However, numerous originals exist to attest to their use. The photographs do indicate that shawls with a large check pattern were relatively popular, as were knitted shawls, both with and without fringed edges.

2 & 3. (Above & below) Scarves, defined as garments in which the length is more than double the width, were made of a varity of sizes and fabrics. Occassionally, they were made of fabrics woven or printed specifically for that use, as with the paisley pattern scarf.

4 & 5. Lace shawls were fashionable in the Civil War. Light lace shawls were worn with dark dresses, while dark lace shawls were worn with both light and dark dresses. The appearance of dark lace over a white fabric (and vice versa) was a popular look of the period, and was also used on parasols and fans.

HEAD WEAR

Bonnets

The variety, trims, and styles of bonnets in the Civil War period are a challenge to classify, as they were an item that women seemed to follow with every whim of fashion. Diaries are full of comments of women altering or re-trimming this, or that bonnet.

The brims of bonnets fashionable at the very end of the 1860s had sides which curved back exposing the face, but were worn a little bit foreward on the forehead. In the 1860s, the brim was taller at the top, but with the sides curving back, the bonnet had a "spoon" shape. The curtain, or gathered piece of fabric at the back of the bonnet, was several inches long at the beginning of the period, but shortened almost to the point of disappearing. Bonnets of the period, like those of ealier years, had a bottom edge which, when viewed from the side, curved downward toward the front edge so that the brim extended several inches lower than the back of the bonnet. This feature did not continue in years after the war.

Decorative ties used on the bonnets were wide pieces of ribbon that tied under the chin. They were supplemented with narrow, functional ties.

1 & 2. At the beginning of the period, bonnets were wide, and relatively low over the forehead.

6. Original bonnet. This bonnet is constructed of alternating bands of woven straw and pink silk fabric. The seams between the two are trimmed with beadwork. The tie ribbons are variegated with shades of pink and rust.

3, 4 & 5. As the war progressed, brims became taller, and trims moved from the sides to the top (often inside of the brim). The brims were cut back at the sides, forming "spoon" shaped bonnets.

Hats

One style of hat which had been popular for some years before the war, and is still seen in some photographs that date to the war, has a relatively low crown. The brim is about half as wide as the crown (when seen from above), and (when seen from the front) slopes downward from the crown. The hats were oval, rather than round.

1. These hats are rather simply trimmed and most often appear to be straw, and were advertised as being especially appropriate for "seaside" trips.

2. (Left) Often they had trim at the front, and ribbons that hung down at the back.

3. Hats were worn straight on the top of the head.

G. G. Fish, Pinx.　　　　　　　　　　　J. P. Soule, Photo.
Entered according to Act of Congress, in the year 1865 by John Soule in the clerk's office of the District Court for the District of Massachusetts.
ON THE BEACH.
Published by John Soule. 14 Summer St., Boston.

4. Lithograph showing women with hats.

The most fashionable women had already discarded the earlier style of hat for all but "seaside" use. Instead, they wore hats with remarkably tall crowns that were squared (not domed) at the top. The crown of these hats curved upward at the side so that they did not sit flat on a table.

1 & 2. The brims of these hats were relatively narrow. Even though the crown narrowed as it approached the top, the brim was less than 1/2 the width of the top of the crown.

3. With the hat sitting on a table, like in this picture, it would rock from side to side.

4 & 5. Hats like this often had more trim than the older style of hat, with contrasting ribbons, and even veils.

There is a third style of hat worn in photographs from the period. However, the vast majority of photographs showing this type of hat have revenue stamps, and therefore date to the last seven months of the war, or the years just after the war. Their use is apparently late-war and post-war, although they appeared in fashion magazines by mid-war.

1 & 2. This hat had a tall crown, and very little brim. It quite often had a decorative rosette or bow of ribbon at the front.

3 & 4. Sometimes these hats were trimmed with feathers which, nonetheless, emphasized the front rather than the side of the hat.

5 & 6. This style of hat usually appeared to be made of cloth, but may be straw, covered with a fabric brim.

ACCESSORIES

Aprons

Aprons followed the lines of dresses, being full at the hips as well as the hem.

1 & 2. Work aprons covered nearly the entire skirt, extending to within inches of the hem. They often had a "pinner" top, which helped to protect the bodice of the gown and were not trimmed. Work aprons were seldom white, but were sometimes made of fabrics with small prints that could conceal the inevitable stains better than white aprons.

3 & 4. "Fancy" aprons were decorative. They extended only 2/3 to 3/4 of the way to the hem. Some of the photographs show "fancy" aprons which are light or white, as well as those that appear to be made of fabrics with a shiny finish, like polished cotton.

Eyeglasses

A close examination of photographs provides evidence of several styles of eyeglasses. Two features of the period are a lack of nose pads and straight temples that did not wrap around the ear.

1. Folding or lorgnette type glasses.

2 & 3. The straight temples are visible.

4, 5 & 6. Generally, the eyeglasses appear to have octagonal or oval frames.

Fans

In the Civil War period, fans were a popular accessory, and there were a number of styles. The fans of this period were much smaller than those of later decades, which sometimes approached a foot in length. In the 1860s, fans were 6-10 inches long when closed.

1. One of the plainer styles of fans was a round palmetto of woven materials. These were generally plain, and were home-made or inexpensive fans.

2. A commercially manufactured round style fan had handles hinged at the center of the circle. The handles were hollow so the accordian-pleated fan folded into the sticks when closed.

3. Fans with feathers at the ends of the sticks were coming into fashion, but fans covered in feathers, or made with ostrich plumes were popular in later decades.

4. Fans of a more traditional shape were often covered with paper or silk, which might be painted or otherwise decorated.

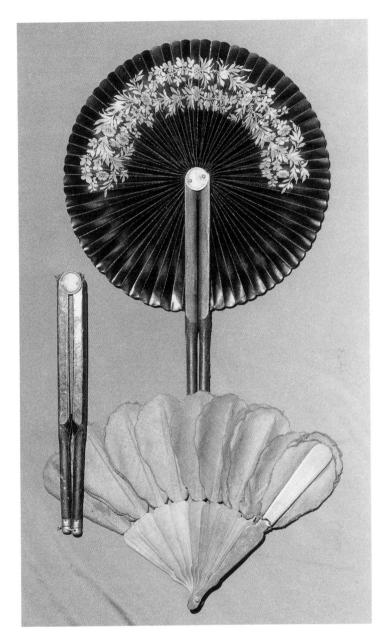

7. Original fans of the Civil War period.

5 & 6. Another popular fan style of the 1860s had oval or leaf-shaped pieces of paper or silk attached to the end of each stick.

Handkerchiefs

The prevalent use of handkerchiefs as a fashion accessory is often overlooked, yet an informal count on accessories revealed that women posed with handkerchiefs nearly as often than they posed with fans, and parasols, and far more often than they posed with reticules.

They were relatively large, about 18" square. As such, these handkerchiefs were smaller than those of earlier periods, and larger than those which followed in later decades.

Handkerchiefs were generally made of fine lawn or muslin (cotton fabrics woven of extremely fine threads). They were usually made of white fabric, although those with striped edges were not uncommon.

Nicer handkerchiefs were trimmed with embroidery. In earlier periods this embroidery surrounded the edge, but by the Civil War, it was often only at one corner. Fashion magazines of the day are filled with embroidery patterns, particularly alphabets for embroidering initials, and with feathers, bees, butterflies, and floral patterns.

1 & 2. When women did not pose with handkerchief in hand, they sometimes arranged them with a corner peeking out of a pocket.

3. Women demonstrated their needlework skills in the fine hemming of their handkerchiefs. Instead of straight hems, some were made with scalloped edges and rolled hems.

4. Handkerchiefs were about 18" square, as such, they were smaller than those of earlier periods and larger than those that followed in later decades.

Jewelry

Entire books could be (and have been) written on the topic of nineteenth century jewelry. Jewelry of the Civil War period was smaller and less bulky than that of later decades in the Victorian era. They were still more bold than delicate, and more geometric than graceful.

Rose gold was particularly popular, and all golds were more common than silvers. (Although there was a brief fad for jewelry of aluminum, which was considered to be a precious metal.) Human hair was woven and arranged into two- and three-dimensional patterns, and was worn in earrings, broaches and bracelets.

1, 2, 3 & 4. (Right) Various examples of jewelry.

Earrings of the period were 3-dimensional designs which dangled from long "French" wires. Safety clasps on wire earrings were not used in this period.

Broaches of the period were large or small. Some (especially cameos) were verticle ovals. Others (especially hair) were horizontal ovals. Broaches of the mid-nineteenth century are often solid in the back, with pins that generally extend beyond the edge of the broach. The hooks were plain "C" hooks without safety clasps.

5 & 6. Human hair was chemically treated, then braided or woven and set in metal frames.

7. Bracelets were extremely popular. They were large, and bold. Some women wore one on each arm, and these bracelets were sometimes (but not always) matched pairs.

8 & 9. (Above & above, right) Watches were worn on long, fine watch chains which permitted them to be tucked in a belt or pocket at the waist. Most watch chains were worn around the neck, extending downward to the waist, however, some simply extended from one side of the belt to the other.

10. (Right) Woman wearing earrings and a broach. Also note pocketwatch suspended from belt.

Parasols and Umbrellas

Umbrellas were known and used during the Civil War period. The difference between umbrellas and parasols is that the umbrellas were very large, and were primarily a masculine accessory. Parasols, on the other hand, were generally rather small.

"Carriage" parasols had a small knob or ring at the top. These sometimes had folding sticks or a hinge in the top of the stick so that the parasol would tilt.

"Walking" parasols were larger and had long pointed finials at the top. Their sticks were long, and rather plain.

The most popular fabric for covering parasols in this period was fine silk or lace. Battenburg lace, and other heavy trims became popular for parasols about forty years after the war. In this period, Battenburg and other tape laces were used for interior decoration, if at all.

Bags and Reticules

Purses, in a variety of shapes and sizes, were popular during decades of the nineteenth century when slender skirts did not permit the use of pockets. During the Civil War, skirts were supposed to lay smoothly over the hoop, which also precluded the stuffing of pockets.

"Miser's purses" or "long purses" as they were known at the time of the Civil War, are believed to have been very popular. They were long, thin, cylinders of net or crocheted work which were closed at the ends. The purse was entered through a slit in the side. Ironically, no photographic evidence was found for them.

Photographs do not provide evidence for the widespread use of drawstring bags in this period. Bags and reticules do not appear in photographs with the frequency of handkerchiefs, fans, or parasols.

Veils

Veils were a fashionable accessory of dress for much of the mid-nineteenth century. During the Civil War they were of such a shape that they hung down from the brim of the hat an equal length all the way around.

The materials from which veils were fashioned varied from fine nets to translucent gauzes to lengths of fabric with crepe or other borders.

While many veils appear to be black in photographs, they were manufactured and worn in a variety of colors. Although the use of black crepe on veils was associated with mourning, evidence suggests that black was a popular color in the Civil War period.

A PRIMER ON HISTORICAL INTERPRETATION

What is Historically Accurate Information?

If the goal of historical interpretation is "to present information that will give the audience a correct impression of the past," then it follows that most of the information presented should represent that which most people were doing. Most of the impressions should represent the "norm," allowing the exceptions to stand out from the rest. Finding the "norm" requires that the following standards be met.

Technical Accuracy: ***Could*** *they have had it?*

Historical accuracy requires that an artifact or style date to the correct period, that it be something similar to that which actually existed, and that it was invented by the period in question. This is the easiest aspect of historical accuracy to research, and it is the area in which the audience most often identifies. "Look—she's got a zipper in her dress. They didn't have zippers, did they?"

Social Accuracy: ***Would*** *they have wanted it?*

Historical accuracy requires that an artifact or style be consistent with the culture of the person being portrayed, and that it be consistent with the times, the place, and the individual. This is a difficult aspect of historical accuracy because researchers tend to impose their own cultural viewpoint on the period. They know that teens wear styles that mature adults wouldn't wear today, but presume that a photograph of a teen from the past is accurate information for the way women of any age dressed in the period. Unfortunately, this leads to gross generalizations. "They all wore hairnets on their hair in that period. See, here's the cover of *Little Women*."

Economic Accuracy: ***Should*** *they have been able to afford it?*

Historical accuracy requires that an artifact or style be consistent with the economy of the person being portrayed, and that it be consistent with the price and value of things at that time. This is something that is often overlooked, because people base their reproductions on the cost of things today, rather than at the time. Today, we tend to think of garments as disposable, rather than planning their modifications for a different dress.

*Is it **Good**?*

Finally, historical accuracy requires than an artifact or style be selected because it will give the audience a good, accurate view of the past, not because the wearer likes it, or because it's unusual enough to ensure that the wearer's photograph will be taken. It should be selected because the wearer can say "yes" to the following question: "Will it give the audience a more accurate impression of the past?"

Where do you get information?

The following are a few tips on doing research, and some suggested sources, along with their benefits and problems:

☞ Always question your sources. Do they list their sources? Are their sources in a position to know? Did your source begin researching with an axe to grind, and, (surprise!!) prove it?

☞ Also question your use of a source. Are you using it because this source is true? ...relevant? ...representative? ...or is it merely available?

☞ One good source can lead to another. Footnotes and bibliographies are gold mines of additional sources.

☞ In addition to visual sources like photographs, lithographs, and paintings, there are also verbal sources like diaries, memoirs, and the fiction published in the period.

☞ Confirm your sources. If you can find only one or only a few sources showing a particular characteristic, don't discard all the negative information. Maybe the characteristic you seek is not representative.

When was a style or characteristic in use?

There is a time lag between the introduction and widespread use of most artifacts or styles. This lag is determined by technology, transportation, and human inclination. The passing of time has proven that fashions come and go. A style originates when it is first adopted by the style-conscious, and those who can afford, and care, to adopt new fashions as soon as they are introduced. It follows, then, that more and more people will adopt the style, until the trend begins to fade and eventually fewer and fewer people adopt the style. Finally, the popularity of the fashion will dissolve, and the highly fashion conscious will have already adopted the next style.

Why bother striving for historical accuracy when it requires so much effort?

Many people bemoan the fact that the "average American" has a poor understanding of the past. Where can they get good information? Others may have non-historical agendas

(like staying on budget, or catering to the egos of stars and their hair dressers when filming). It falls to the living historian, whose only goal is to impart correct information, to strive for historical accuracy, despite the effort.

In the long run, historical accuracy is cheaper than the alternative! Because folks at the time of the Civil War were generally very economical and took great effort to make their clothing durable, making and using historically accurate clothing is generally less expensive than making and using inaccurate reproductions. For example, modern costumes are often destroyed as the hems drag along the ground, absorbing mud and fraying the fabric. This is much less a problem when a hem protector braid is sewn to the outside of the hem, and when the dresses are hemmed off the ground, as most were at the time of the Civil War.

Finally, studying and accurately reproducing the lives of our ancestors better acknowledges the hard work and challenges that they faced than fictionalizing them as people who lived in a mythological world where money was not an issue, and people were simply modern Americans wearing "quaint" clothing. It's time to stop ignoring women's history, but it's not time to create myths about it.

Beware of Research-by-Modern-Interpretation. *Using images to describe period behavior is subject to errors. The modern mind may read different meanings into the photographs.*

How?

How can you work toward historical accuracy without turning your whole life (and income) over to it?

☞ Find out if something is accurate *before* you buy it: Don't be a: "Fast And Researchless Buyer" (FARB)

☞ Remember the goal: Go for the norm.

☞ Work for accuracy, then strive for perfection: Concentrate on the obvious and the visual first.

☞ Put on a new head, not just a new hat. Think like the person you're portraying: Acquiring a wardrobe was a process, not an event.

☞ Hair and makeup are just as important as clothing.

☞ Avoid caricatures and myths like the plague. They are contagious.

Beware

Beware of "Research-by-Selected-Source." Sources gathered because they show a specific characteristic, but do not reflect the entire population.

Beware of "Research-by-Sole-Source." Finding a style in one (or a few) sources does not necessarily indicate common use.

Beware of "Always" or "Never" Statements. There is an exception to every rule.

Beware of Research-by-Banquet-Menu. Certain styles were more commonly worn by women of some ages than by others.

Beware of "Research-By-Hearsay." Often it's not history, but myth-story.

Common Sources

Auto-biographies

☞ Be aware the economic bias: whose stuff gets written and published?

☞ Be aware of hidden agendas of writers, even unconscious ones. People write about what they perceive as important in their lives (social contacts, not soap-making).

☞ Many never-published works are coming to light. Beware of modern editing which may introduce a bias, or misinterpretation of old terms and phrases.

Journals, Letters

☞ Be aware of the social bias: Whose papers were saved and donated to libraries?

☞ Understand that people tend to write about the unusual.

☞ Modern editors sometimes delete the very day-to-day information we want!

Beware of "Research-by-Sole-Source." *Finding a style in one (or a few) sources does not necessarily indicate common use. If this were an "occupational photo of a loan-shark," it hardly proves that all loan-sharks wore a shark's jaw on their head.*

Non-fiction

☞ Look for public documents like a local census, newspaper, almanac, books of receipts and compiled knowledge.

☞ Don't overlook local histories and special-topic histories.

Periodicals

☞ Look for local publications, contemporary dates and retrospectives ("year in review") as well as national publications from the date. Be aware of editors' and publishers' goals and marketing programs.

☞ History magazines tend not to check every fact or opinion. They think the writers know the topic, or they wouldn't be publishing the writing! Factual inaccuracies slip by, as do insupportable conclusions, opinions, and impressions.

Mentoring, Gossip, Hearsay

If you find someone from the period still around, and willing to divulge information, call the tabloids.

Mentoring can be a God-send if the mentor is well-informed and objective. Formalized "mentor" programs are an excellent way to inform those new to the topic. However, the pitfall of research-by-hearsay is that the source of the information may have an agenda. Indicating that "I sell the best white snoods" does not tell the listener that white snoods

were seldom worn. "Here's a hat just like the one I wear" doesn't tell the listener whether the hat is correct. "Everyone in our unit wears lace collars" doesn't help the listener to know that the entire unit is perpetuating a myth.

Fashion plates

They're accessible: Publications containing fashion plates are available in many library loan programs. Plates have been reprinted for decades.

Be aware of the economic bias, time lag from introduction of a fashion to adoption by the population, and modifications made between high fashion and daily use. Modern eyes tend to interpret details differently than eyes contemporary to plates.

Lithographs/art-work

Look to find local artists; often they date their works. They aren't always trying to portray reality (but sometimes do it by accident).

Beware of "Research-by-Invention-Date." *The fact that something (like a Greek chiton) had been invented or existed by the time of the war doesn't mean it was in widespread use.*

Photographs

Especially helpful for seeing artifacts/garments as they were worn and used, in combinations, and by whom they were used. Can be dated with relative precision. Make sure topic is comparable to that being studied (i.e. geography, age, sex, social and economic status, type of event).

Original garments

These are particularly helpful for seeing colors and construction details, and can be accurately dated. However, the piece has to be dated to its latest (most recent) feature. The original style and early alterations are often no longer visible. Unfortunately, with an original, you cannot see the fit or coordination of the piece, and we tend to over-accessorize and over-trim.

Beware of "Research-by-Gross-Generalization." *The man in the lower right is Edwin Hutchinson, member of a reknown family of singers. However, the existence of a photograph of people in 1830s clothing including this singer is not necessarily an indication that other performers (and certainly not* **all** *performers) wore these costumes with any regularity.*

As in any area of research, those who are most knowledgeable often have strongly held, differing views. Historical research is a process of interpreting clues. The text contained in this book is the author's interpretation of the clues provided by thousands of sources.

The conclusions for this book were largely derived from a survey of photographs from the period. That research was augmented—and substantiated—by studying original garments and by reading diaries, jounals, and memoirs of women in the period. Through the study of originals, constructional details were studied, and through the readings information was gathered on women who may not have had their photograph made. Emphasis was also placed on the readings which mentioned economic and wartime hardships. A suggested reading list follows.

THE "LOOK OF THE PERIOD" FOR WOMEN OF ALL AGES

THE "LOOK OF THE PERIOD" FOR WOMEN OF ALL AGES

THE "LOOK OF THE PERIOD" FOR WOMEN OF ALL AGES

VARIATIONS ADOPTED BY YOUNG AND MORE FASHIONABLE WOMEN

VARIATIONS ADOPTED BY OLDER AND MORE CONSERVATIVE WOMEN

CONSERVATIVE APPAREL

LAVISH APPAREL

THE "LOOK" FROM THE BACK

❖ SUGGESTED READING LIST ❖

Ames, Mary. *From a New England Woman's Diary in Dixie in 1865.* Springfield, MA. The Plimpton Press. 1906.

Baird, Nancy Chappalear, editor. *Journals of Amanda Virginia Edmonds, Lass of the Mosby Confederacy, 1859-1867.* Stephens City, VA. Commercial Press, 1984.

Boykin, Laura Nisbet and Mary Wright Stock, editor. *Shinplasters and Homespun, The Diary of Laura Nisbet Boykin.* Rockville, MD. Printex, 1975.

A Lady of Virginia (Judith White McGuire Brockenbrough) *Diary of a Southern Refugee, During the War.* New York, NY. E.J. Hale & Son 1867.

Buck, Lucy Rebecca. *Sad Earth, Sweet Heaven, The Diary of Lucy Rebecca Buck During the War between the States.* Birmingham, AL. The Cornerstone, 1973.

Clark, J. Mat. *Luella Blassingame: The Blue and the Gray.* Nashville, TN. McQuiddy Printing, 1903.

Cruse, Mary A. *Cameron Hall, The Story of the War.* Philadelphia, PA. J.B. Lippincott & Co., 1867.

Darrah, William C. *Cartes de Visite: In Nineteenth Century Photography.* Gettysburg, PA. William C. Darrah, 1981.

Dawson, Sarah Morgan. *A Confederate Girl's Diary.* New York, NY. Houghton Mifflin, 1913.

Hague, Parthenia Antoinette Vardaman. *A Blockaded Family, Life in Southern Alabama during the Civil War.* New York, NY. Houghton Mifflin, 1888.

Johnston, Mary Tabb. *Amelia Gayle Gorgas, A Biography.* University, AL. University of Alabama Press, 1978.

Kelbaugh, Ross J. *Directory of Civil War Photographers.* Baltimore, MD. Historic Graphics, 1993. Lancaster, Dallas M. and Mary H., editor. *The Civil War Diary of Anne S. Frobel of Wilton Hill in Virginia.* Birminghan, AL. Birmingham Printing and Publishing Co., 1986.

A Lady *The Workwomen's Guide.* Reprinted Guilford, CT. Opus Publications, 1986.

Lander, Ernest McPherson, Jr. and Charles M. McGee, Jr., editor. *A Rebel Came Home, The Diary and Letters of Floride Clemson 1863-1866.* Columbia, SC. University of South Carolina, 1989.

Lawrence, Catherine S. *Autobiography: Sketch of Life and Labors of Miss Catherine S. Lawrence.* Albany, NY. James B. Lyon, 1896.

Loughborough, Jas. M. *My Cave in Vicksburg, with Letters of Trial and Travel.* Spartanburg, SC. The Reprint, 1976.

Massey, Mary Elizabeth. *Ersatz in the Confederacy, Shortages and Substitutes on the Southern Homefront.* Columbia, SC. University of South Carolina, 1993.

Miers, Earl Schenck, editor. *When the World Ended, the Diary of Emma Le Conte.* Lincoln, NE. University of Nebraska Press, 1957, 1987.

Morrill, Lily Logan, editor. *My Confederate Girlhood, the Memoirs of Kate Virginia Cox Logan.* Richmond, VA. Garrett & Massie, 1932.

Richards, Caroline Cowles. *Village Life in America 1852-1872.* New York, NY. Henry Holt & Co., 1913.

Sartain, James Alfred. *History of Walker County Georgia, Volume 1.* Carollton, GA. A.M. Mathews, 1972.

Smedes, Susan Dabney, and Fletcher M. Green, editor. *Memorials of a Southern Planter.* New York, NY. Alfred A. Knopf, 1965.

Swint, Henry L., editor. *Dear Ones at Home, Letters from Contraband Camps.* Nashville, TN. Vanderbilt, 1966.

Welton, J. Michael, editor. *My Heart is so Rebellious, the Caldwell Letters, 1861-1865.* Warrenton, VA. Fauquier National 1991.

Woodward, C. Vann and Elisabeth Muhlenfeld, editor. *The Private Mary Chesnut, the Unpublished Civil War Diaries.* New York, NY. Oxford University, 1984.

Wright, D. Giraud. *A Southern Girl in '61, the War-Time Memories of a Confederate Senator's Daughter.* New York, NY. Doubleday, Page & Co., 1905.

INDEX